Inventive Wire Weaving

20+ UNIQUE JEWELRY DESIGNS

Susan Barzacchini

KALMBACH BOOKS

WAUKESHA, WISCONSIN

This book is dedicated to two men: Michael Barzacchini,
my loving husband, a man of grace, gratitude, and
wisdom; and Jonathan Barzacchini, our son. My heroes.

Kalmbach Books
21027 Crossroads Circle
Waukesha, Wisconsin 53186
www.JewelryAndBeadingStore.com

Published in 2018
22 21 20 19 18 1 2 3 4 5

Manufactured in China

ISBN: 978-1-62700-495-4
EISBN: 978-1-62700-496-1

Editor: Erica Barse
Book Design: Lisa Schroeder
Photographer: William Zuback
Proofreader: Annie Pennington

Library of Congress Control Number: 2017941417

Contents

Foreword

My friend Susan is an artist. Her intricate, yet fluid style, attention to excellence and innovative details stand her work apart from ordinary craft. Yet, the Susan that I have grown to know is a born teacher, too. Susan has a passion for sharing and encouraging. She is able to communicate her ideas in a way that excites and inspires you. Her manner of instruction is succinct, yet all-encompassing. I have every confidence that the dear reader will be driven to achieve their own artistic goals through Susan's passionate tutelage. Wrap on!

— Tela Formosa, jewelry artist

Open the door to possibilities and take that journey to astonish the world with your wire-weaving art within. Reveal the extraordinary within your spirit.

~ Susan

4

Introduction

Art is a giving and receiving world of imagination and connections. It is a cycle of being mentored, and then becoming the mentor. It is a place where puzzle pieces are put together and a vision is revealed. The art form of weaving wire, of gently sashaying wire curls through your fingers, can be mastered through experience and dedication. This book was written to inspire you and to ignite your own path toward making wire-weaving discoveries. This medium is not just art; it also opens doors to healing and cathartic therapeutic time spent with self and others. It tends not to be something that is rapidly created, as weaving wire takes time and concentration. It truly is a dance with fingers and mind.

The pages of this book contain a variety of projects that teach each reader how to weave wire and work with metals and natural elements. You will learn how to channel-set a gemstone, drill a larger hole in a pearl, solder a jump ring, snap-set a gemstone, and even how to imprint a delicate cicada wing into a layer of metal—in addition to learning how to weave wire. Each piece is my own design, and I challenge you to deviate from the step-by-step and explore variations of the projects.

— Susan

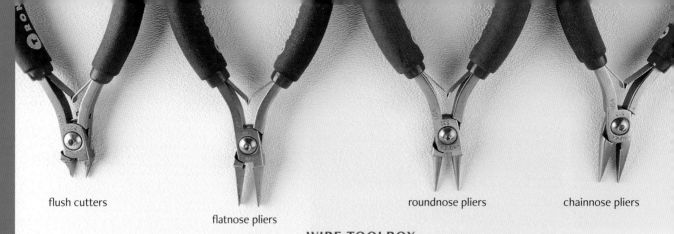

flush cutters

flatnose pliers

roundnose pliers

chainnose pliers

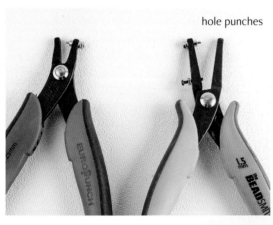

bail-forming pliers

WIRE TOOLBOX

Flush cutters (I prefer Tronex® Razor Flush® cutters), flatnose pliers, roundnose pliers, and chainnose pliers are the most essential tools when weaving wire. The chainnose and flatnose both allow for making bends in metals and wire, as well as gripping wire. The roundnose is used for making loops and soft arches. The flush cutters cut a clean, straight end off of wires. Flush cutters with a narrow point are perfect for cutting thinner gauge wires very close to the weave. High-quality and close-cutting flush cutters are essential for achieving a finished look in woven wire.

Heavy-duty roundnose and chainnose pliers have more strength than traditional pliers to bend and loop heavier gauges of wire.

Bail-forming pliers are perfect for making consistent and uniform loops.

hole punches

Hole punches are a great alternative to drilling in metals. They create a clean hole in metals, which are perfect for weaving through with wire. The size of punch I use most is the 1.25mm punch.

Nylon-jaw pliers help to restore wire to a straight position when it is kinked or bent needlessly. I prefer to straighten wire with my fingers, but occasionally, the thicker-gauge wires need a little more resistance that these pliers offer.

Micro-needle chainnose pliers are very helpful for tucking wires and getting into tightly woven areas.

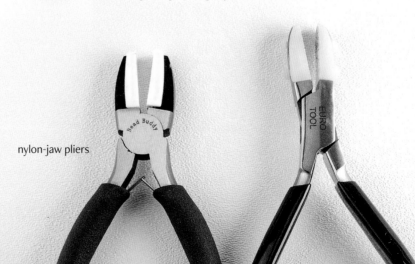

nylon-jaw pliers

I frequently use temporary blue painters tape, a permanent marker, tape measure, ruler and shape templates at the bench. The blue tape is perfect for holding metals together, holding wire down while marking, holding wires together, and aligning stamp positioning. The permanent marker is used to mark wire and metal measurements, and can be easily removed with rubbing alcohol.

A steel bench block is made from a metal that is harder than non-ferrous metals, such as copper, silver, and gold. This makes it a perfect tool for flattening wire and texturing metal when used in combination with a hammer. I use a chasing hammer to spread and flatten metal. Keeping the hammer face smooth is essential for smooth flattening of wire and metals. The ball-peen, or small rounded face of the chasing hammer, is used for riveting and for texturing metals. Rawhide hammers allowing you to strike wires and metals without damaging the metal surface. I use the rawhide hammer when dapping metal with a wooden dap to prevent the wood from becoming damaged.

steel bench block

rawhide hammer

chasing hammer

Wire mandrels, stepped roundnose pliers, wooden dowel rods, and cuticle sticks are just some of the wire-forming tools that I use to create a round wire frame or shape. The wire mandrels are made from steel and make an excellent tool for coiling wire.

CraftOptics™ magnifying telescope glasses assist in clearly seeing very thin gauges of wire. Besides the nimbleness of my fingers, this is my favorite tool to use while wire wrapping.

A straight pin (shown with a bead tray, below) is used to open an existing tight weave while allowing for threading of thin gauge wires through the weave. It is also used to help with re-threading 28-gauge wire through a bead so the wire doesn't kink.

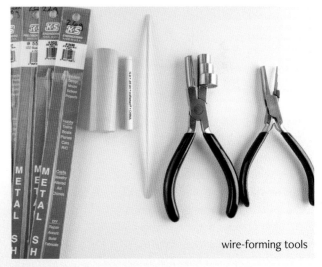

wire-forming tools

magnifying telescope glasses

bead tray

straight pin

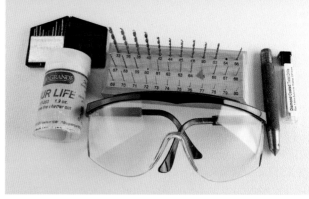

DRILL TOOLBOX

Mini drill presses have a controlled mechanism to smoothly glide up and down on a stationary column while the piece remains stable. Placing a slab of wood as a buffer on the drilling table allows the drill bit to penetrate through the metal and then the wood. A drill press uses a chuck and chuck key to remove and replace drill bits.

Assorted drill bits, drill bit lubricant, center punch and safety glasses are all essential tools to have while using the mini drill press. An assortment of twist and diamond twist drill bits allow for creating tiny holes in metals for weaving. The lubricant is a waxy substance that helps to improve performance and extend the life of a drill bit by reducing friction. It is also used with burs and disk cutters and most processes that create friction. A center punch, when hammered into metal on a steel bench block, creates a divot that allows the drill to pierce the metal in the correct spot. Safety glasses are a must while working with the drill, as drill bits can break and metal debris can fly with the rapid rotations of the drill. Also, tying back long hair and pulling up sleeves is another safety precaution required while drilling.

FINISHING AND POLISHING TOOLBOX

A cushioned fingernail file, #0000 steel wool, a half-round metal file, liver of sulfur, and polishing cloths are all finishing tools that give the metal a finishing glow. Liver of sulfur darkens copper and silver to a gunmetal gray. A drop in a disposable cup of very hot water, followed by dipping the metal into the mixture will darken the metal. I rub the surface of the woven wire with the steel wool to highlight raised portions of the piece after a patina. The final step is polishing the work with a chemically impregnated polishing cloth. Sanding sponges in various grits are perfect for rounding wire ends, smoothing wire following hammering, and for removing tool marks on the wire.

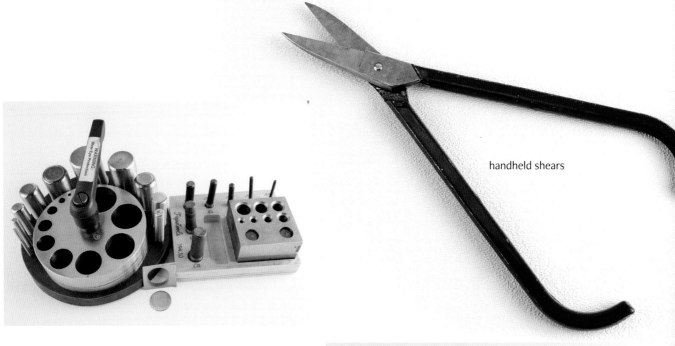

handheld shears

DISK CUTTING AND DOMING METAL TOOLBOX

A disk cutter cuts perfectly round disks from sheet metal. The disk cutter comes with various sizes of circular punches. Use a heavy brass mallet to strike the cutter, and use a wax lubricant.

A doming block and dapping tools dome circular metal disks by putting the disks into a well of the block and hammering a corresponding dapping tool on top of the disk.

Handheld shears cut metal similarly to the way scissors cut paper in a straight line or a slight curve. Shears can be used as an alternative to metal sawing as long as the curve is not too tight. They can also be used to cut a metal circle by first drawing a circle with a template and then cutting it out with the shears.

METAL STAMPING TOOLBOX

A brass hammer, assortment of letter stamps, patterned stamps, and grid stamp guides are used to create words, patterns, or textures on metals and wire. The brass hammer is a softer metal than the stamps and thus allows for a perfect bite into the stamp when striking. Using a metal working hammer can cause damage to the stamp and tends to bounce off of the stamp. Quality stamps make all the difference when aligning and obtaining a clean stamped image.

Texture stamping tools are a great way to repeatedly and quickly create a texture on the metal. This hammer grips a metal stamp by way of inserting and twisting the bottom knob.

SOLDERING TOOLBOX

A paintbrush, easy silver solder in wire form, flux paste, cross-locking tweezers in a third hand, copper tongs, a Solderite board/brick, a butane torch with fuel, and pickle in a pickle pot are all tools necessary for soldering. I find that triple-filtered butane aids in keeping the torch valve from becoming clogged. The torch that I use is a large butane torch, which works well to anneal and solder small pieces. Copper tongs are used to remove and place soldered pieces into a crock pot filled with warmed pickle (not shown), which is used to remove surface oxidation. Using steel tongs will charge the pickle and cause silver pieces to have a thin copper coating. Flux is necessary to allow the wire solder to flow. The Solderite pad protects your work surface by reflecting heat. Many projects require the use of a third hand tweezers to hold objects while being soldered.

ADDITIONAL WIRE AND METAL TOOLS

Place anti-tarnish strips in a sealed plastic zipper bag to prevent metals from tarnishing during storage.

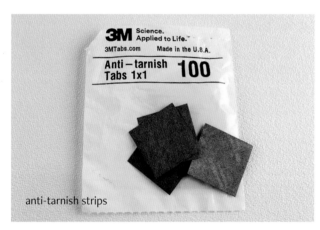

anti-tarnish strips

Riveting hammers spread the ends of thick-gauge wire to create a rivet. Methodically hammer both ends of the thick wire to secure two pieces of metal together.

Ring mandrels are used to size ring shanks; they also make a great circle-forming tool. Necklace mandrels help to shape neck cuffs into an anatomically correct form. Place wire or metal onto the mandrel and forge the metal against the mandrel with a hammer.

Bolt cutters are a fast way of cutting spoon and fork handles when creating jewelry from cutlery. Alternatively, use a jeweler's saw to cut the handle.

Two-part epoxy is used to secured half-drilled pearls to a wire peg. It is a very strong glue that must be mixed in equal parts for about a minute.

Engraving pens are used for signing a piece of work on the back. I use this tool to trace around a hammered leaf or bug wing impression, which allows the detail to show readily in a piece. It is used just like a pen on flat metal or wire.

ring mandrels

WIRE

The wire used in this book tends to be fine silver or dead-soft copper wire. There are two reasons why I use fine silver instead of sterling silver. First, fine silver creates a smooth ball at the end when heated with a torch, while sterling silver tends to dimple. Sterling is made of an alloy of copper and silver, and the two have different melting points; dimpling occurs due to the difference in response to temperatures during torching. The second reason I use fine silver is that it is more malleable than sterling silver, making it perfect for weaving. Wire used in this book is non-ferrous, meaning that it is free of iron and resists rusting and corrosion. Ferrous metals commonly have magnetic properties and are harder than non-ferrous metals. While wire measurements are carefully calculated, tension, wire breakage, and finger-hold may require extra wire. Please allow for additional wire lengths with each project, if needed.

WIRE GAUGE

I typically use 16-, 18-, 20-, and 28-gauge wire. Gauge refers to the thickness of the wire. The higher the number, the thinner the wire. For example, 28-gauge wire is thinner than 16-gauge wire.

WIRE HARDNESS

Wire hardness comes in hard, half-hard, and dead-soft. Each has a place in wirework. I use hard wire when making jewelry components that have to have a firm framework, such as earring wires. Half-hard wire also makes a nice firm framework and holds a great right-angle bend for square or angled pieces. Dead-soft wire is the easiest to arch, circle, twist, and manipulate when weaving and creating loops.

Wire can also be work-hardened. This means that wire can become more rigid and strong after hammering, bending, drawing against metal, or using a metal tool upon the wire. Work-hardening is frequently done when creating wire frames to offer additional stability to the frame. Work-hardening has its limitations, however. While working metal, the crystals within the metal become tighter—and thus harder—and can cause the metal to break when overly worked. Work-hardening can be reversed by torch-annealing the metal, thus relaxing the crystal structure within the metal.

bolt cutters

two-part epoxy

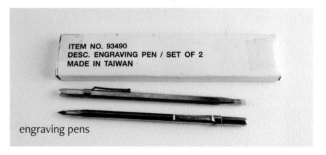

engraving pens

SOFT FOLD

Soft folds are used with arabesque shapes and other shaping steps. Using flatnose pliers, bend the wire 180 degrees using the jaw of the flatnose pliers as a sort of gap-stop for the other side of the wire.

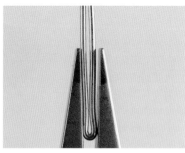

HARD FOLD

There are several places in the book where a "hard fold" is required. This indicates that the wire is folded at a specified location using flatnose pliers, and then the fold is compressed tightly with the flatnose pliers, creating a tighter fold.

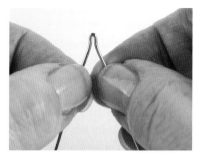

ARABESQUE WIRE SHAPE

There are many opportunities to create an arabesque shape in the book. This shape begins by hard- or soft-folding a wire, opening up the fold, and wrapping the two sides of the wire around a mandrel or dowel.

TORCH BEADING A WIRE END

The ends of both fine and Argentium silver wires bead (ball up) beautifully when the wire is held perpendicular to and just in front of the inner blue cone in the flame of a torch.

The flame causes the metal to melt and retract into a ball. These beaded ends add an element of interest in wire projects.

ANNEALING

When the metal becomes work-hardened, it will need to be annealed so that it can be further formed into various shapes. This is done by heating the metal to a specific temperature with a torch just in front of the blue-cone flame.

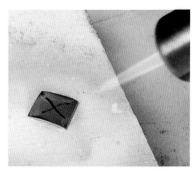

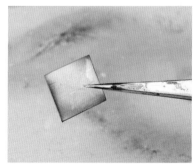

Begin by marking an "X" on the metal to be annealed with a permanent marker. The "X" will serve as an indicator that the annealing has been reached and the process is complete when it virtually disappears while being torched.

SECURED BASIC LOOP

The beauty of this loop is that since it is coiled closed, it won't open during wear. Cut a 24-gauge wire about 10cm long, and use chainnose pliers to make a 90-degree bend at about 4cm.

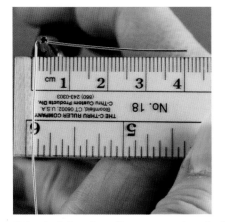
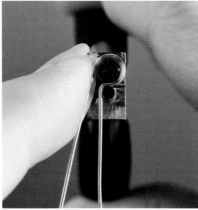
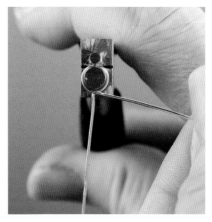

Using bail-forming pliers, create a loop by forming the wire around the jaw of the pliers with your index finger until the top wire length meets the bottom wire length.

Then, flip the bail-forming pliers 180 degrees to allow room for the shorter wire length to cross over the longer wire length, forming a right angle.

Hold across the loop with the tips of chainnose pliers, and coil the shorter length of wire around the base of the loop and continue downward.

Coil three times, and then use flush cutters to cut the wire.

SECURED BEAD

Securing a bead helps to stabilize it and fill spaces between the bead and the frame wires. Begin by coiling twice on both sides of the frame and bring the wire ends up and next to the beads.

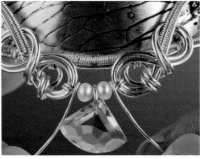

Pull the wires down on both sides of the bead.

Coil two times next to the bead on the wire that the bead is strung upon. Trim the wire at the back of the coil.

BRIOLETTE WRAP AND DANGLE

The briolette wrap technique requires some practice. Use copper wire to practice the wrap until the process becomes familiar. This mini tutorial demonstrates how to create the wrap and make a dangle, which is used in many projects in the book.

Cut a piece of 22-gauge wire 25cm long, and bend it at 5cm.

String the briolette on the wire, and bend the wire up at the other side of the stone.

With the tips of the chain-nose pliers, bend the longer wire inward (about 4mm from the bead top) toward the shorter wire.

Bend the shorter wire at a 90-degree angle to the long wire at the location of the bend, forming a triangle.

Hold across the triangle shape with the tips of the chainnose pliers, above the briolette, and coil the short wire end at the top.

Make three coils.

String three or four beads on the long wire, and bend the wire at a right angle to the beads.

Make a loop with a 3mm bail-forming pliers or round-nose pliers about 1mm from the beads.

Insert the loop through a loop at the bottom of the piece.

With the tips of the chain-nose pliers, grasp the loop and make about three coils below the loop.

SOLDERED RING

This technique can be used to solder a jump ring or other pieces of wire.

To make a jump ring, coil 16-gauge wire onto a mandrel so it wraps around at least two times.

Flush-cut the rings about 1mm from the end. Note the flat part of the wire cutters is facing the ring. This is important, as this will give a flush or flat, smooth cut.

Flip the rings upside-down and flush-cut the other end of the wire in line with the first, leaving two straight wire ends.

Flush-cut the center of the coil, and close the ring with two pairs of flatnose pliers.

Mark the seam so it is easier to visualize where the soldering process will take place.

Place the ring on a Solderite board or a firebrick, and brush a small amount of paste flux on the seam.

Place two small pieces of easy solder wire on either side of the seam on top of the ring.

Use the torch to torch the ring, starting at the back away from the seam, and then evenly heat the sides. Just as the flux begins to turn clear and glassy, heat the seam. The metal must be evenly hot for the solder to flow across the seam. Quench the ring in water, place it in pickle to clean it, and sand the seam smooth.

DRILLING METAL WITH A DRILL PRESS

Drilling with a drill press allows for piercing of metals so that wire can be "sewn" onto the metal. It is also used for riveting, cold and hot connections, and ornamentation. A mini drill press is my preferred method for drilling; however, a variable-speed flexshaft or hand drill may also be used. Use various sizes of drill bits to create different-sized holes.

Mark the metal with a permanent marker at the location of the desired drill hole, and hammer a divot at the mark with a center punch. The divot helps the drill bit to bite into the exact location needed.

Lubricate the drill bit with BurLife to extend the life of the bit.

Put on safety glasses, tie back long hair and loose clothing, and put the metal on top of a slab of wood. Turn the power on and pull down the drill lever. Lower the motor down the column until the drill bit comes into contact with the divot in the metal. Drill completely through the metal.

DISK CUTTING

The metal disk cutting tool has a two-layer platform with multiple holes and several corresponding cutters to make a variety of sizes of disks from metals up to 16-gauge thickness.

Lubricate the disk cutter of your choice with a lubricant like BurLife. Put the cutting platform on a rubber mat or piece of leather. Open the platform. Put the sheet metal between the two platforms of the disk cutter, making sure to completely cover the desired hole size, and then close the platform tightly on top of the metal. Place the cutter in the corresponding hole and with the flat, angled end facing down, strike the cutter with a brass hammer until the disk falls out of the bottom of the platform.

Push the cutter through the platform, and retrieve the disk.

DISK DOMING

Place a metal disk in the doming block. With a rawhide mallet, strike fairly hard onto the disk with the rounded portion of the dapping punch against the disk.

Move the dap slightly in several directions to create a uniformly domed disk.

STAMPING WORDS ON METAL

Before stamping, it helps to write out the word on paper. The space between words counts as a letter space, so include it in your written words. When writing out your word, put a mark on top of the letter that is the center of the word/words, as this is the starting point for stamping.

Begin by marking the middle of the metal stamping blank, and draw a horizontal line across the metal where the each of the bottoms of the letters will rest. Note that stamping is started at the middle to give the word symmetrical spacing to the left and right of the word. Use a metric ruler to help with placement of the stamps. Tape the ends of the stamping blank to a steel bench block. Use a brass hammer to stamp the first letter at the middle mark and on the horizontal line with one firm strike. Line up the second letter on the horizontal line and about 2mm from the edge of the previous letter. Again, strike once to the top of the letter stamp with the brass hammer. Stamp the other letters to the right and then the left of the middle mark, making sure to stay on the horizontal line.

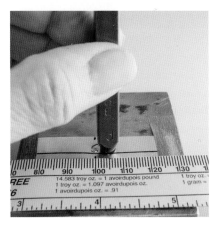 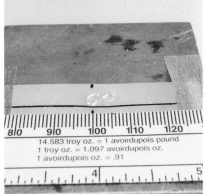 

ENLARGING A PEARL HOLE

When enlarging a pearl hole, wear protective glasses and a facemask. Pearl hole enlargement, as outlined in this book, is a technique for pre-drilled pearls only and not intended to be done with stone, glass, or plastic beads—nor is it intended to be used to start a fresh hole in a pearl. Insert a drill bit with a larger diameter than the existing pearl hole into a drill press. Secure the pearl in the pearl vise with the existing hole facing up through the vise hole.

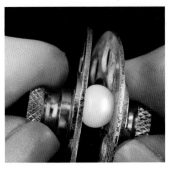 

Tighten the upper and lower screws on the pearl vise to clamp down on the pearl. Rest the vise at the edge of a wooden board, bring the drill bit down to the existing hole on the pearl, and slowly drill through the pearl. If drilling a half-drilled pearl, drill only halfway through the pearl.

TEXTURING METAL WITH STAMPS

A texturing metal stamper is a great tool for obtaining an all-over texture on the surface of sheet metal and thick gauge wire. Insert a 6mm metal stamp into a slot at the top of the hammer, and lock it in place with the knob at the bottom. Repeatedly strike the metal in a random manner.

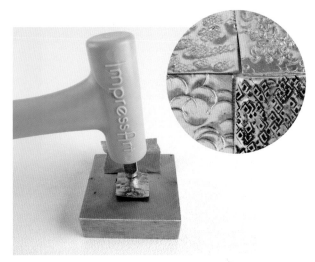

This type of texturing affords a number of options for patterns based on the number of patterned metal stamps you own that fit into the hammer.

PATTERNING METAL WITH BRASS PLATES

Patterning metal with this technique renders metal with a similar appearance as having been rolled in the rolling mill. Note that after this vigorous hammering, the metal will need to be annealed, especially if any further forming of the metal is needed. With temporary blue painters tape, tape the metal to be imprinted onto a bench block.

Note that tape should only be at the edges, as it will leave a print on the metal when hammered. Put the patterned brass sheet on top of the metal with the pattern side down.

Tape the brass onto the bench block and use a household hammer to vigorously strike over the entire surface.

Leave one piece of tape attached to the brass, like a hinge, and lift it up to see if the pattern is complete. If the pattern is not complete, re-tape the brass, and hammer again. Anneal the copper.

CONTINUOUS LOOPS

The method of continuous-looping allows the jewelry artist to add a sort of lacy appearance to their jewelry. It is also a great way to make multiple loops to add fringe and frame beads. You'll need 24- or 22-gauge dead soft wire, fine silver wire, or copper wire and bail-forming pliers (size varies depending on loop size needed).

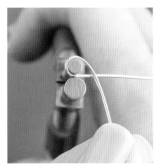

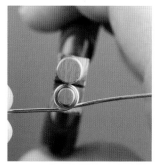

FIRST LOOP

Decide where the first loop will be located on the wire and mark this place. Put the barrel of the bail-forming pliers on this mark, with the desired plier barrel on top of the wire. Gently close the pliers on the wire.

Wrap the wire around the top barrel, stopping when the wire reaches the bottom barrel. Notice how the large barrel is on the bottom in this example.

Flip the two barrels around so the bottom barrel is on top and the desired barrel remains in the loop. Complete the loop by continuing to wrap around the desired barrel.

The first loop is completed when both tails are extending almost in a straight line from both sides of the bottom of the loop.

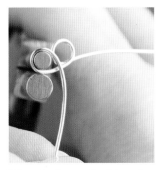

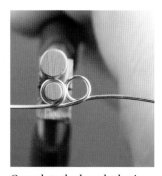

SECOND LOOP

Place the desired barrel of the pliers about 2mm distance from the first loop on the long tail. The large barrel is again on the bottom.

Wrap the long tail of the wire up and over the top of the desired barrel. Stop when the wire reaches the bottom barrel.

Readjust the bail barrels so the bottom barrel is now on top and the desired is on the bottom, keeping it within the loop.

Complete the loop by letting the side of the loop touch the first loop slightly. Bring the tail around to form a straight line with the tail on the other side of the first loop.

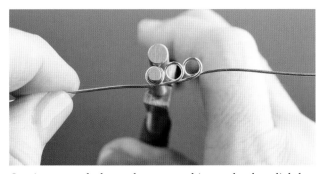

Continue to make loops that are touching each other slightly.

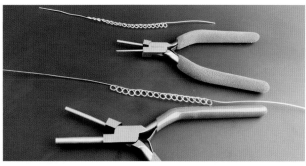

Here are two examples of the size of loops made by different sizes of bail-forming pliers.

WEAVING BASICS
2-1 WEAVE

The 2-1 weave is a tidy weave, as the weaving wires line up beautifully, especially on thinner gauge wire. Demonstrated below is the 2-1 weave on two wires, but this weave also looks beautiful on rows of multiple wires.

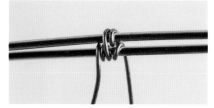

Coil the weaving wire two or three times around the lower frame wire. Wrap the weaving wire around both the upper and lower frame wires, and then bring the wire end in between the two frame wires. Coil once around the upper frame wire.

Bring the weaving wire to the back and under the lower frame wire and coil around the lower frame wire one time.

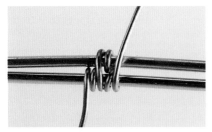
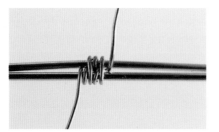
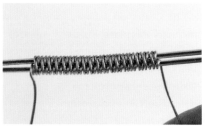

Bring the weaving wire up in front of both frame wires.

Wrap the weaving wire around the upper frame once, and pull it up between the two frame wires.

Continue the sequence of wrapping around both frame wires once and coiling around each frame wire once.

MODIFIED FIGURE-8 WEAVE

This is a nice, tight weave that pulls wires close together.

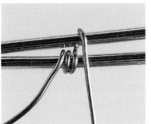
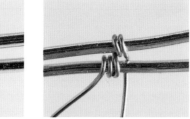
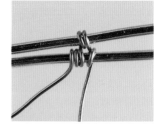

Coil around the first frame wire three times. Add a second frame wire. Bring the weaving wire behind and on top of the second frame wire. Bring the weaving wire between the two frame wires, and make a coil on the upper frame wire.

Pull the weaving wire up and over the upper frame wire, and insert the weaving wire between the two frame wires.

Bring the weaving wire under and around the lower wire in a coil.

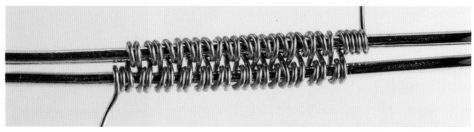

Bring the weaving wire in between the two frame wires and behind the upper wire. Continue with the sequence for a full row of weaves.

DOUBLE-UP/SINGLE-DOWN WEAVE

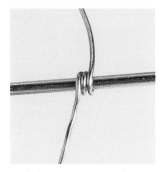

Coil the weaving wire three times on the first frame wire.

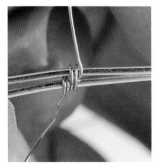

Add a second frame wire above the first, and wrap the weaving wire around the first and second frame wires two times. Bring the wire end between the first and second frame wire.

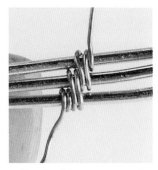

Add a third frame wire, and wrap around the second and the third frame wires. Bring the weaving wire end between the second and the third frame wires twice.

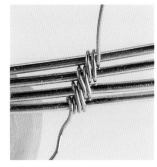

Add a fourth wire, and wrap around the third and fourth frame wires. Bring the weaving wire end between the third and fourth frame wires twice.

Add a final fifth frame wire, and wrap around the fourth and fifth frame wires. Bring the weaving wire end between the fourth and fifth frame wires twice.

Coil the weaving wire around the top frame wire and between the third and fourth frame wires.

Coil around that frame wire, and then bring the weaving wire down between the next two frame wires.

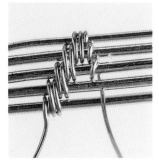

Coil around that frame wire, and bring the weaving wire down between the next two frame wires.

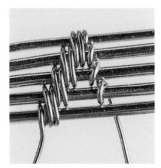

Coil around that frame wire, and bring the weaving wire down between the next two frame wires. (You have reached the first frame wire.)

Coil around the first frame wire.

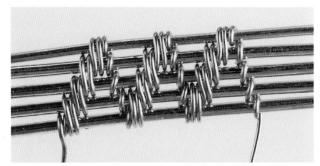

Wrap the wire around the first and second frame wires twice, and repeat the previous steps.

JEWEL BEETLE
WING EARRINGS

Nature meets fashion with these brilliantly iridescent jewel beetle wings.
This lesson demonstrates how to stack jewel beetle wings on top of
each other for a sort of "fish scale" chain mail effect. These wings can
be drilled easily and add a pop of color when used in jewelry designs.

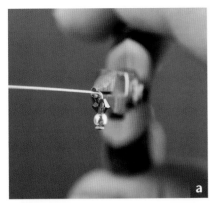

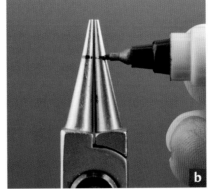

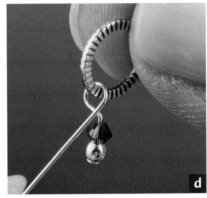

SUPPLIES

- o **2** sterling silver headpins at least 1½-in. long
- o **2** 2mm round sterling silver beads
- o Pair of sterling silver earring hooks
- o **6** 4mm 18-gauge twisted or plain sterling silver jump rings
- o **8** 3.2mm 22-gauge sterling silver round jump rings
- o **2** 10mm closed patterned rings
- o **2** 3mm bicone or round faceted crystals
- o **4** 4cm jewel beetle wings (large)
- o **4** 3cm jewel beetle wings (medium)
- o **4** 2cm jewel beetle wings (small)

TOOLS

- o Needle chainnose pliers
- o Chainnose pliers
- o Roundnose pliers
- o Flush cutters
- o Drill and drill bit, size #56

1 / Make crystal dangles

String a 2mm sterling silver round bead and a 3mm crystal on a headpin, and bend the headpin wire above the beads at a 90-degree angle with needle chainnose pliers **(photo a)**. Mark an area on the roundnose pliers with a permanent marker to use as a guide to keep the loops the same size on both earrings **(photo b)**. Make sure the loop is at least 3mm to allow the crystals to move freely. Line the roundnose pliers mark up with the tail of the bent headpin wire, and bring the tail of the headpin up and over the roundnose pliers barrel at the mark **(photo c)**.

2 / Continue the earrings

Slightly open up the loop, and place a 10mm closed ring in this loop **(photo d)**. Using needle chainnose pliers, hold across the loop and wrap the tail of the headpin around the base of the loop at least twice **(photo e)**. Flush-cut the excess wire and tuck the wire end (see "Secured Basic Loop," p. 13). Add a 3.2mm jump ring to the loop of the dangle **(photo f)**.

3 / Drill holes on the wings

Drill holes in the top of each beetle wing with a #56 drill bit **(photo g)** (see "Drilling Metal with a Drill Press," p. 16). This size drill bit will allow the jump ring to pass through the hole.

4 / Attach wings to jump rings

Place a 4mm twisted jump ring through the holes in two large beetle wings. The brown undersides of the beetle wings should be facing each other **(photo h)**. Close the ring and make sure the wings move freely on the jump ring **(photo i)**.

23

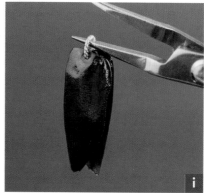

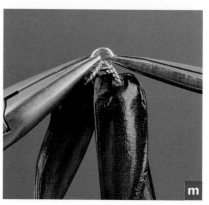

5 / Work in chain mail

Add 4mm twisted jump rings to the other beetle wings: Join a medium pair and a small pair of wings **(photo j)**. Insert a 3.2mm ring through the twisted ring (large wings), leaving it open **(photo k)**.

6 / Attach the medium wings to the large wings

Add the closed twisted ring (medium wings) to the open 3.2mm ring, with the undersides of the wings fitting over the large wings like a hat **(photo l)**. Close the 3.2mm ring **(photo m)**. The large and medium set of wings are now secured together with two twisted rings and a 3.2mm ring **(photo n)**. Add a 3.2mm ring to the twisted ring (medium wings), leaving it open **(photo o)**.

7 / Attach the small wings to the medium wings

Add the twisted ring (small wings) to the open 3.4mm ring **(photo p)**, and close the ring. Attach the twisted ring (small wings) to a closed 10mm patterned jump ring with a 3.4mm ring **(photo q)**. Attach an earring wire to the top 3.2mm ring holding the crystal. Repeat to make a second earring.

JEWEL BEETLE WING NECKLACE

What is this "jewel" beetle bug? Elytra is the name for hardened upper wings of beetles that provide a protective barrier for flight wings. The elytra of the jewel beetle have been used ornamentally in ancient as well as modern times. You may substitute any dangle bead you like in this versatile design.

SUPPLIES

- 13cm 16-gauge round fine-silver wire
- 196.5cm 20-gauge round fine-silver wire
- 81cm 24-gauge round fine-silver wire
- 671cm 28-gauge round fine-silver wire
- 12.5cm sterling silver 2mm bead chain
- 18 in. sterling silver 2mm round rolo chain with clasp (cut at center of chain)
- **17** 3mm round sterling silver beads
- **2** 8mm ornate round sterling silver beads with hole to fit 20-gauge wire
- **9** 3.2mm 22-gauge sterling silver jump rings
- **9** 6mm round crystals or beads
- **18** 3x4mm saucer crystals or beads
- **19** 3mm bicone crystals or round beads
- **9** 1–1¼ in. jewel beetle wings

TOOLS

- Micro-needle chainnose pliers
- Chainnose pliers
- Flush cutters
- 2.5mm and 3.5mm bail-forming pliers
- Permanent marker
- Tape measure
- Sanding stick
- Drill and drill bit, size #60
- Finishing and Polishing Toolkit (optional)

1 / Make large continuous loops

Cut 58.5cm of 20-gauge wire. Leave a 13cm tail from one end of the wire, and begin creating 17 continuous loops with 3.5mm bail-forming pliers (see "Continuous Loops," p. 19). (The 13cm tail on either side of the loops will be used later.) Use a permanent marker to mark the middle (9th) loop.

2 / Make small continuous loops

Cut 42cm of 20-gauge wire. Leave a 6cm tail, and create 19 continuous loops with 2.5mm bail-forming pliers. Make a small mark on the middle (10th) loop.

3 / Prepare the base

Cut three 32cm pieces of 20-gauge wire. These wires will become the base for the

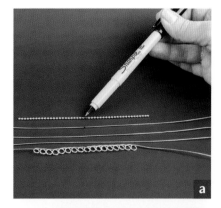

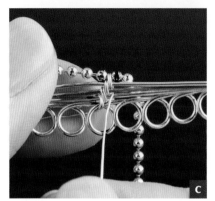

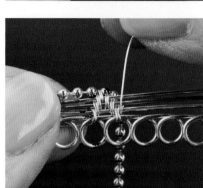

weave. Mark the middle of these wires. Mark the center of the 12.5cm bead chain. Cut 191cm of 28-gauge wire, and mark the center. Arrange and reference wires and bead chain as follows:
Bottom: large 3.5mm continuous loops (loops facing down)
First: 20-gauge wire
Second: 20-gauge wire
Third: 20-gauge wire
Top: Bead chain **(photo a)**

4 / Begin the weave

You will be making a mountain-valley weave; the peaks are the mountains and the valley looks like a "V." Beginning at the middle of the 191cm 28-gauge wire, begin your mountain-valley weave at the middle of the 3.5mm continuous-loop wire and the middle of a 32cm piece of 20-gauge wire. Wrap twice around the middle loop and the 20-gauge wire. Place a second 20-gauge wire on top of the first 20-gauge wire, and wrap twice around the first and second wire. Bring the 28-gauge weaving wire between the first and second base

wires **(photo b)**. Place a third 20-gauge base wire on top of the second 20-gauge base wire, and loop twice around these two wires. Bring the weaving wire between the second and third base wires.

5 / Add the bead chain

Catch the middle of the bead chain between beads with the weaving wire, and wrap twice around the bead chain and the third base wire. Bring the weaving wire between the first and second base wires **(photo c)**. Continue the double-wrap downward to the right on all base wires, and catch the next continuous loop at the bottom **(photo d)**.

NOTE: Catch all of the continuous loops with the weaving wire.

Finish the mountain-valley weave to the last continuous loop on the right and left sides, and end with two coils on the first base wire. Gently bend the woven wires into an arch around a can or bottle **(photo e)**.

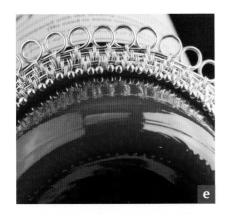

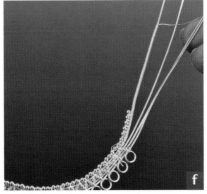

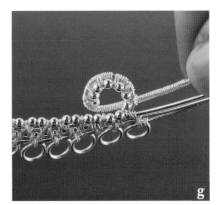

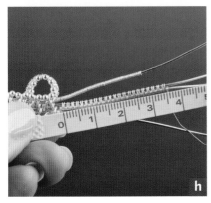

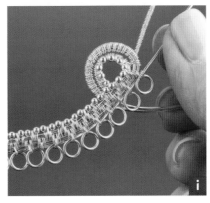

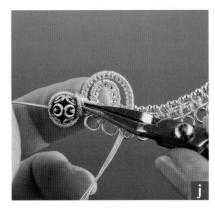

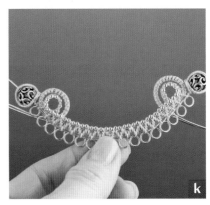

6 / Continue the necklace

Cut two 72cm pieces of 28-gauge wire. Coil one piece around the third base wire two or three times on the right side of the weaving. Alternate between coiling on the third base wire and catching in between each bead of the beaded chain with two wraps. After all the chain has been woven, continue coiling for 4cm past the chain on the third weaving wire (photo f). Repeat on the left side with the other piece of 28-gauge wire.

7 / Add the end loops

Gently arch the coil and the tail of the bead chain by hand into a counter-clockwise loop on the right side of the coil (clockwise loop on the left side). Bring the coiled tail behind the loop and parallel to the second base wire (photo g).

8 / Make more loops

Cut two 61cm pieces of 28-gauge wire. Coil twice on the first straight 20-gauge wire on the right, and then wrap the first

and second wire twice. Continue this coil two-wrap two pattern for a total of 3.5cm (photo h). Repeat on the left side with the second 61cm piece of 28-gauge wire. Wrap these coil two-wrap two wires around the wire-and-chain loop, ending with the wires trailing down behind the second-to-last continuous loop (photo i).

9 / Add a large bead

String an ornate 8mm bead on the tail of the continuous-loop wire on the right side. Push the bead against the last loop of the continuous loops. Wrap the coiled wire around the ornate bead, starting at the top of the bead and circling clockwise around the bead (counter-clockwise for the left side). Wrap the tail of the coiled wire twice around the base between the bead and the woven loop, and cut the wire in the back. Tuck the cut end around the coil using micro-needle chainnose pliers (photo j). Repeat on the left side (photo k).

10 / Continue weaving

Using 2.5mm bail-forming pliers, make a loop on the far side of the 8mm bead. Insert the end link of one half of the rolo chain onto the loop. Secure the loop by wrapping once at the base and then bringing the tail under the coiled loop around the bead. Then, pull it up and toward the bead loop (photo l). Continue to wrap the tail around the base of the loop. Cut and tuck the excess wire (see "Secured Loop," p. 13).

11 / Connect the pieces

Bring the two tails of the coil-two/wrap-

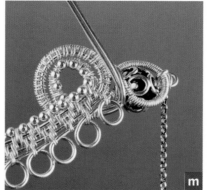

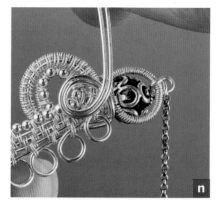

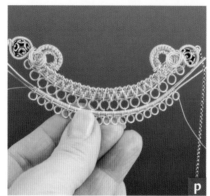

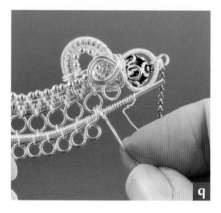

two wire weave under and between the last continuous loop and the bead **(photo m)**. Make a counterclockwise loop (clockwise on the left side) with your fingers; keep the two wires side by side. Bring the tails of the two wires up to the top between the bead and the woven loop **(photo n)**. Bring the tails behind the woven loop, and wrap both wires around the left side of the base of the woven circle one time. Tighten that wrap gently with needlenose pliers. Trim and tuck wires in back **(photo o)**.

12 / Add a new wire

Cut 13cm of 16-gauge wire. Cut 132cm of 28-gauge wire. Beginning in the middle of the 28-gauge wire, coil twice onto the midpoint of the 16-gauge wire. Place the 16-gauge wire below the large 3.5mm continuous loops and catch the middle continuous loop with the 28-gauge wrapping wire, one time. Coil two more times on the 16-gauge wire and then place the small 2.5mm continuous loops (with loops pointing downward) under the 16-gauge wire,

and wrap the middle loop on the small continuous loop. Continue coiling on the 16-gauge wire and alternating one wrap around the upper and then the lower continuous loops. Leave the last two upper continuous loops unwrapped. Wrap the left side as well **(photo p)**. Continue coiling down to the ornate bead on both sides of the 16-gauge wire with the 28-gauge wire.

13 / Finish the frame

Bend the right tail of the small lower continuous loop up at a right degree angle toward the second-to-last upper continuous loop, with chainnose pliers. Wrap the tail of the small lower continuous loop around the second-to-last large upper continuous loop twice **(photo q)**. Trim and tuck the excess wire. Using chainnose pliers, grasp the very end of the 16-gauge tail, and turn it down and around into a tight loop. Use a sanding stick to sand some of the sharp edges of the 16-gauge wire ends, and tuck the end **(photo r)**.

14 / Add more beads

Cut 41cm of 28-gauge wire. Coil three times onto the outer left side of the upper large continuous loop. Make sure the wire is coming up and in front of all the continuous loops. String a 3mm sterling silver bead on the 28-gauge wire, and frame the bead into the far left large continuous loop. Bring the 28-gauge wire on top and into the second continuous loop. Pull the wire behind the two loops and up through the first loop and then in front of the second loop **(photo s)**. Add a second 3mm silver bead to the 28 gauge wire, and frame the bead into the second loop. Repeat across the entire upper continuous loop, ending with three coils onto the right outer loop. Trim and tuck the excess wire **(photos t and u, front and back)**.

15 / Finish the necklace

Apply a patina, buff with #0000 steel wool, and clean the entire necklace (optional). Cut 41cm of 28-gauge wire. Attach 3mm bicone crystals to the

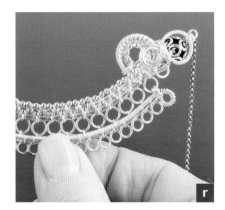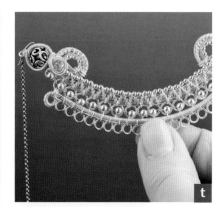

smaller lower continuous loops in the same manner as the upper continuous loops **(photo v)**. Using a drill and #60 drill bit, drill a hole at the top of each jewel beetle wing from the underside of the wing. Add a 3.2mm jump ring to each of the drilled wings, leaving the rings open.

16 / Add finishing touches

Cut nine 9cm pieces of 24-gauge wire. Make a basic loop on each wire. On each wire, string a saucer crystal, a 6mm round bead, and another saucer bead. Make another basic secured loop, but don't finish the wrap **(photo w)**. Attach a wing to the secured loop with the jump ring. (The largest wing is located at the center and the remaining wings become slightly smaller toward the ends.) Make sure the top loop is perpendicular to the bottom loop of the stacked crystals. Secure the largest wing component to the center small lower continuous loops. Continue to add a wing component to every other continuous loop. Adjust to make sure the wings lay flat.

design variation

Don't have bug wings? Use a variety of dagger beads or use the "Briolette Wrap and Dangle" technique, p.14, to create a dangle fringe instead.

CHAKRA TREE OF LIFE PENDANT

Chakra-colored stones and an arabesque frame
of this tree of life is what makes this piece unique.
This lesson outlines one way to make shapes
out of wire in the form of an ornate frame,
but the instructions can be used for outlining
most shapes.

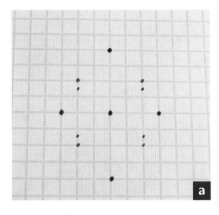

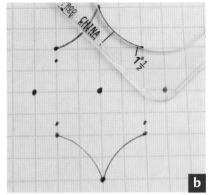

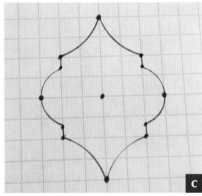

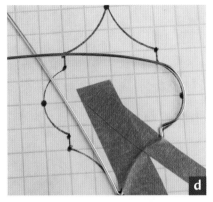

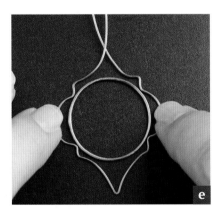

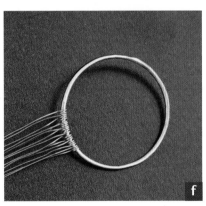

SUPPLIES

o 12cm 18-gauge dead-soft round wire

o 210cm 26-gauge dead-soft round wire

o 80cm 20-gauge dead-soft round wire

o 220cm 28-gauge dead-soft round wire

o **2** 3mm metal beads

o 6cm bead chain with 2.4mm beads (total of 20 beads)

o Graph/grid paper (four squares per inch)

o Temporary blue painters tape

o Rock bead chips in red, orange yellow, green, blue, indigo, and violet (or desired)

TOOLS

o Wire Toolkit

o Hammer

o Steel bench block

o Dowel 1 in,/25mm

o Permanent marker

o Soldering Toolkit

o Circle templates, inches or millimeters

1 / Make the pattern

Mark grid paper following as shown in the photo **(photo a)**. Create an arch from the top dot to the red dots above and below using a 1½-in. (3.8cm) circle template **(photo b)**. Create a small, straight line from each of the arches (red dot) down a half of a square at all four corners. Using a ⅞-in. (2.4cm) circle template, connect the small lines in a semi-circle on the left and right sides **(photo c)**.

2 / Create the frame shape

Cut 40cm of 20-gauge wire. Make a soft fold in the 20-gauge wire at the halfway point, so it follows the shape of the point at the bottom of the pattern (see "Soft Fold," p. 12). Tape the wire down to the right of the lower point on the pattern. Make a bend at each dot/corner with chainnose pliers. After each bend, tape the wire down to the right of the bend to support the shape during subsequent bends **(photo d)**. Your entire frame will be taped down with several pieces of tape by the end. Lock the shape in place by gently hammering on a steel bench block.

3 / Center the circle for the tree

Cut 12cm of 18-gauge wire. Using a 1-in. (2.5cm) dowel, create a circle with the wire around the dowel. Overlap the wire ends, and draw a line where the wires intersect with a permanent marker. Remove the wire from the dowel, and flush-cut both marks on the wire to make a circle. Solder the circle closed and hammer it slightly to work-harden it (see "Soldered Ring," p. 15). Make sure the circle fits into the arabesque frame so the circle edges touch the four inner corners of the frame **(photo e)**.

4 / Make the tree trunk base

Cut seven 30cm pieces of 26-gauge wire. Fold all seven wires in half in a soft fold. Hook each of the seven folds onto the ring, and coil three times onto the ring, one at a time, beginning at the fold **(photo f)**. Twist pairs of the 26-gauge wires together, leaving a wire on either end untwisted **(photo g)**. Flip all of the wires into the center of the ring. Twist all the wires together to make the trunk. To make the large branches of the tree, divide the 26-gauge wires into

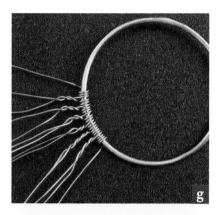

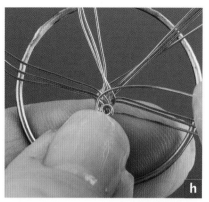

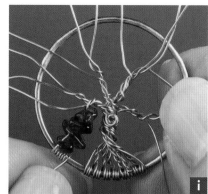

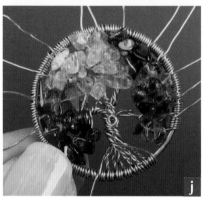

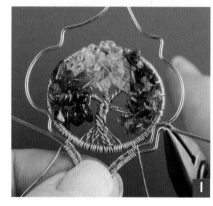

groups of two and three, making sure to leave one wire separate. The extra wire is used to make a knothole in the tree trunk: create a small loop with the tips of your fingers or fingernails, and then swirl the wire around the loop once or twice and work it back into the trunk with the other wires (**photo h**). Then, twist the sets of large branch wires two or three times, separate them into single wires, and spread them around the ring.

5 / Add the rock bead chips

I used garnet, amber, citrine, peridot, sodalite, iolite, and amethyst chips (in that order). Starting at the far left side of the ring, place enough beads onto the first wire to fill the space between the twisted branch and the ring, and then make five or six coils to the right of the beads (**photo i**). Continue adding various colors of beads to the small branches, and always coil to the right of the beads. Once all the beads are added, continue coiling around the ring to fill in the blank spaces. There will be a gap of uncoiled area to the far right

of the circle (**photo j**). Cut one of the remaining 26-gauge wires, and use it to fill that gap with coils. Bring all the wires to the back of the ring, and cut them very close to the inner back of the ring. Tuck the ends if needed.

6 / Weave the arabesque frame

Cut 220cm of 28-gauge wire. String a 3mm bead onto the center of the wire. Nest the bead inside the lower peak of the arabesque frame, and coil twice to the left and right of the peak. Soft-fold a 40cm piece of 20-gauge wire at its midpoint, and place it under the lower peak of the arabesque form; leave about 1cm between the lower peak and this wire's fold.

NOTE: The remaining actions outlined in this step are completed on both the left and right sides of the frames.

Wrap the weaving wire around both the arabesque and the outside frame wires three times, ending with the weaving wire between the two frame wires.

Coil three times onto the outer frame. Continue with this wrap-three/coil-three pattern until you reach the point where the ring meets the weave. Wrap the weaving wire around the tree circle and inner frame twice (**photo k**). Bend the outer frame so it follows the inner arabesque frame at each angle (**photo l**). Coil around the entire outer corner until you reach the half-circle in the arabesque frame, and then wrap twice around both frame wires, followed by wrapping twice on the inner wire and the ring. Wrap twice around the inner and outer frame wires (**photo m**). Continue to bend the outer frame around the arabesque frame so the shapes follow each other.

Add a 3cm piece of bead chain: Wrap twice around one end of the chain, between two beads, then coil a few times the outer frame until you reach the space between the next two beads (**photo n**). Continue for the rest of the bead chain; connect the outer frame to the arabesque frame at the first bead

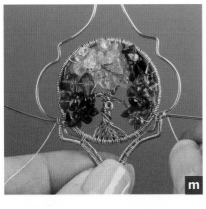

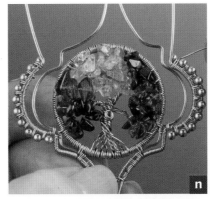

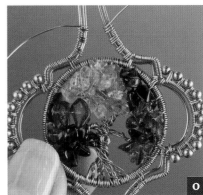

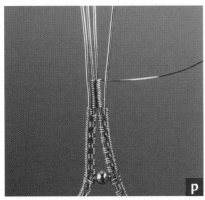

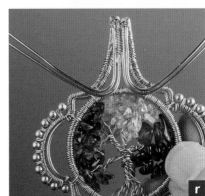

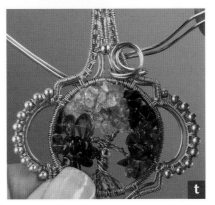

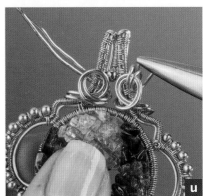

with two wraps. Continue the weave around the frame as you did at the first half of the frame **(photo o)**. Attach a 3mm bead to the inside of the inner wires with the weaving wire.

7 / Create the bail

Continue weaving the wrap-three/coil-three (six pairs) pattern up the bail wires. Wrap the weaving wire 15 times around the two inner bail wires **(photo p)**. Using your fingers, bend the bail weave to the back, beginning at the fifth pair of three/three weaves **(photo q)**. Keep the wires parallel. Arch both

pairs of the unwoven bail wires upward in the back of the piece, so the bottom of the arch is just at the level of the circle **(photo r)**. Bring the bail wires to the front, and make an outward loop with both pairs of wires **(photo s)**. Bring the bail wires in front and under the 3mm bead, and thread to the back **(photo t)**. Trim some of the wires to pass the remaining wires through the circle you just made more easily. Coil the wires onto the top of the previous loop **(photo u)**. Cut the wires close to the back and tuck, as necessary **(photo v)**.

LOTUS FLOWER PENDANT

The lotus flower is rooted in mud and has a stalk that reaches the top of the water, revealing a lovely flower unscathed by the muddy waters. In various parts of the world, the lotus symbolizes purity and beauty. There is a mystic beauty in this flower with its arabesque petal shape, which translates beautifully into wire shapes.

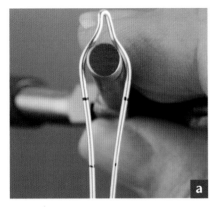

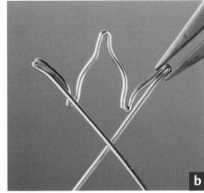

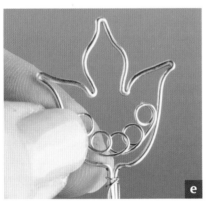

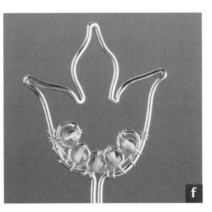

SUPPLIES

- o 30cm 18-gauge dead-soft round wire
- o 15cm 16-gauge dead-soft round wire
- o 80cm 20-gauge dead-soft round wire
- o 20cm 22-gauge dead-soft round wire
- o 2.6m 28-gauge dead-soft round wire
- o 10cm 24-gauge dead-soft round wire
- o **2** 6mm OD metal soldered jump rings
- o 2.5cm bead chain
- o **5** 3mm round stone beads
- o **1** 2mm metal bead
- o **2** 3mm metal beads
- o **1** 10x5mm top-drilled briolette
- o 12.5cm cable or rolo link chain*

TOOLS

- o Wire Toolkit
- o Permanent marker
- o 11mm, 13mm, and 32mm dowels
- o 1.5mm, 3mm, and 6mm bail-making pliers
- o 600-grit sandpaper

The links need to fit 22-gauge wire.

1 / Create the lotus flower

Hard-fold 30cm of 18-gauge wire in half (see "Hard Fold," p. 12). Using a permanent marker, mark 1.5cm from the fold, and then mark 1cm from the first mark. Open up the fold and use a 6mm mandrel or 6mm bail-making pliers to form a petal shape below the fold (see "Arabesque Wire Shape," p. 12) **(photo a)**. Bend up at the first mark on either side of the wire, and pull the folds open. Using chainnose pliers, bend down on the second mark on both sides, and compress slightly on the fold **(photo b)**. Open up that fold. Using an 11mm dow-

el, form the bottom of the lotus flower by crossing the flower wires underneath the dowel **(photo c)**. Mark on the wires where they cross over at the bottom of the dowel. Use chainnose pliers to bend each wire downward, so that they are parallel to each other to create the stem of the flower **(photo d)**. Create five continuous loops (see "Continuous Loops," p. 19) with 10cm of 22-gauge wire and 3mm bail-forming pliers. Curve the continuous loops inward so they fit the inside base of the lotus **(photo e)**. On the left side of the lotus frame, attach the connecting loops to the base of the

lotus with 25cm of 28-gauge weaving wire: Wrap two coils onto the lotus frame followed by one wrap around the frame and the first continuous loop, string a 3mm bead, wrap one time at the top of the loop, wrap one time between the first loop and the second loop, wrap around the base of the second loop and the lotus frame, and continue this wrapping until all five continuous loops have a bead. Finish with two coils on the lotus frame on the right side, and cut the weaving wire ends **(photo f)**. Using chainnose pliers, bend the stems up at the base of the lotus up the back of the

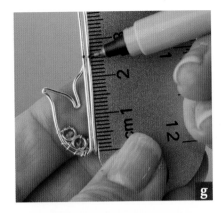

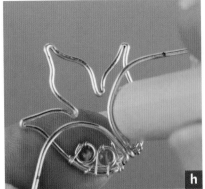

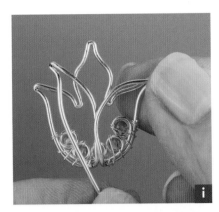

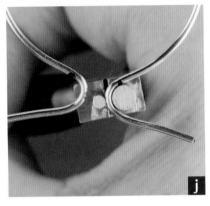

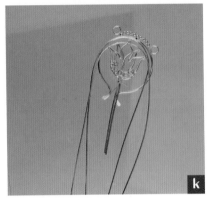

flower, and mark 2.5cm from that bend on both the left and right wires (back of piece) **(photo g)**. Using a 13mm dowel, arch both the left and right wires outward **(photo h)**. Hard-fold downward at the mark on each wire, and then open up those folds to create secondary lotus petals on the back of the flower **(photo i)**. Bring the wires down to the base of the flower, and bend them down so they are parallel again. Wrap a scrap piece of wire around the top of the stem wires a few times to keep them closed.

2 / Make the circle frame

Create a circle with a 32mm dowel and 15cm of 16-gauge wire. On the 16-gauge wire, mark where the wires cross over on the dowel. Bend the ends of the wire outward on the mark with 6mm bail-forming pliers **(photo j)**. Cut the wire ends 5mm from the bend on the left and right side. Hammer the end of the wires flat on a bench block, and sand the ends so they are smooth and rounded. Place two 40cm pieces of 20-gauge wires (arched at their mid-

point) inside the 16-gauge wire circle. Place the lotus inside of the arched 20-gauge wires. Place the bead chain on top of the 16-gauge circle and one soldered jump ring at each end of the bead chain **(photo k)**.

Make a tassel: Make half of a secured loop with 10cm of 22-gauge wire (see "Secured Basic Loop," p. 13). Thread five 2.5cm pieces of chain onto the loop, and secure the loop. Add a 3mm bead, and make a 1.5mm secured loop above it **(photo l)**. Set the tassel aside.

Begin the weave: Cut a 1.8m length of 28-gauge weaving wire and mark at the middle of the wire. Beginning at the mark, wrap the center of the beaded chain to the top of the 16-gauge circle. Add the first 20-gauge wire, and wrap the weaving wire around the 16-gauge circle and the center of the 20-gauge wire. Add the second 20-gauge wire, and wrap it to the first 20-gauge wire. Wrap the weaving wire around the peak of the lotus and the second 20-gauge wire

(photo m). Weave upward with single coils on the two 20-gauge wires and the 16-gauge circle. Wrap around the 16-gauge circle and the space between the beads in the bead chain. With the left side of the weaving wire, repeat to weave down and around the 16-gauge circle and the two 20-gauge wires. Wrap the left weaving wire around the second 20-gauge wire and the peak of the lotus **(photo n)**.

Continue this weave (see "2-1 Weave," p. 20) to the end of the ball chain, and then double-wrap a soldered jump ring onto the top of the 16-gauge circle. Continue the weave down to the left and right lower lotus petals, and wrap the peak of the lower petals to the second 20-gauge wire twice. (The back lotus petals are not included in this weave.) Continue the wrap-two/coil-one pattern to about 1cm from the bottom bends on the 16-gauge stem wires **(photo o)**.

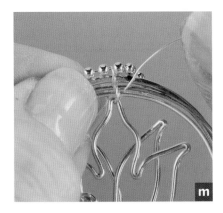

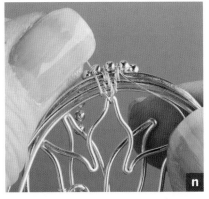

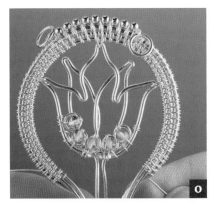

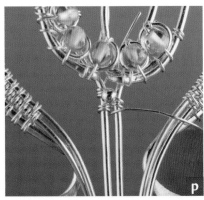

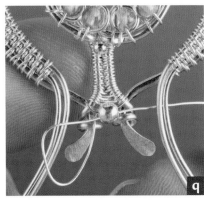

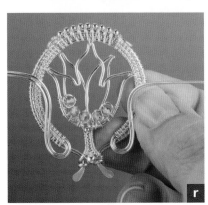

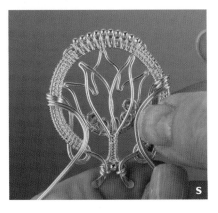

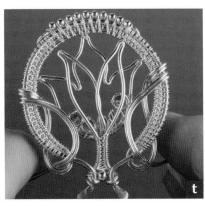

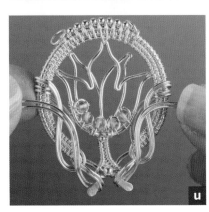

3 / Weave the lotus stem

Cut 45cm of 28-gauge wire, and coil three times on the left stem wire at the base of the lotus. String a 2mm metal bead onto the wire, and begin a modified figure-8 weave on the left and right stem wires (see "Modified Figure-8 Weave," p. 20) **(photo p)**. Continue the modified figure-8 weave to about 5mm above the bends at the ends of the 16-gauge circle. Bring the left and right stem wires around the left and right bends, and coil once around them. Continue the 28-gauge weave to the 16-gauge arches. String a 3mm metal bead onto the wire, thread it between the stem wire loops on the opposite side, and coil a few times to secure **(photo q)**. Cut the weaving wire and stem wire ends.

4 / Create ornate side wires

Gently curve the left and right 20-gauge frame wires up, in, and then outward just below the bottom lotus petal with the tips of your fingers or rounded fingernail **(photo r)**. Wrap the 20-gauge wires around the woven frame one full turn, keeping the wires side by side during the wrap. Bring the wires to the back of the piece. Arch the 20-gauge wires in and out, using your fingertips to create the arch **(photo s)**. Insert the 20-gauge wires into the left and right lower loops **(photo t)**. Bring the 20-gauge wires in front of the left and right forged wire ends, and loosely circle around them. Arch the wires inward, up, and toward toward the lotus **(photo u)**. Coil the left and right 20-gauge wires around the woven frame, keeping the wires parallel, and bring all of the 20-gauge wires to the back of the weave. Cut the ends of the 20-gauge wire, and tuck **(photo v)**.

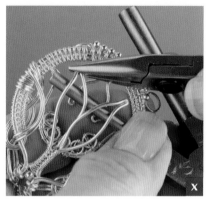

design variation

You can create the bail to enhance a different pendant altogether—or simply mix your metals, as in this copper version of the piece.

Attach the tassel with 10cm of 24-gauge wire by coiling on either side of the 20-gauge wire that is wrapped around the forged wire ends **(photo w)**.

5 / Finishing touches

Slide a 6mm mandrel or pliers under the back lotus petals, and pull down on the tips to bow out the petals backwards (back of the piece) **(photo x)**. Attach a briolette at the top petal of the lotus using 10cm of 28-gauge wire, and make a secure loop on either side of the briolette **(photo y)**.

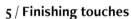

1 / Making the bail peak

Cut 18cm of 20-gauge wire, and hard-fold the wire in half. Mark 1.5cm from the fold on both sides of the wire, and mark 1cm from those marks **(photo a)**. Open the folded wire and form an arabesque shape with a 6mm mandrel or bail-forming pliers. Bend outward on either side of the peak at the 1.5cm mark

(photo b). Hard-fold inward at the next mark on both sides of the wire **(photo c)**. Open up the last hard folds to form downward-facing peaks **(photo d)**.

2 / Making the bail loops

Cut 18cm of 20-gauge wire. Mark at 8cm, 9cm, and 10cm on the wire, with the 9cm mark in the center of the wire. Bend up at a 90-degree angle on the 8cm and 10cm marks. Mark about 2mm above the bend on both sides. Place bail pliers at the 2mm mark and curve the wire around the bail pliers until it makes a closed loop **(photo e)**. Repeat on the

other side. Bend the wire outward on either side of the loops so all straight parts of the wire are in the same plane **(photo f)**.

3 / Weaving the bail

Cut 80cm of 28-gauge wire (weaving wire). Starting in the center of the bail, wrap the center of the weaving wire around both the bail wire and 18cm of 20-gauge wire. Add 18cm of 20-gauge wire, and wrap around the two wires. Wrap once around each of the three wires. Mark where the bail peak will fit onto the weave on the left and right

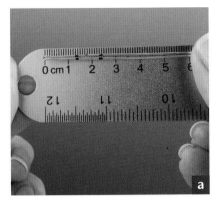

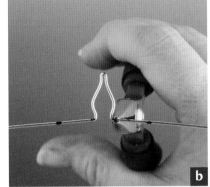

SUPPLIES (BAIL)

o 72cm 20-gauge dead-soft round wire
o 20cm 22-gauge dead-soft round wire
o 90cm 28-gauge dead-soft round wire
o **1** 4mm bead
o **2** 3mm metal beads

TOOLS

o Wire Toolkit
o 3mm bail-forming pliers

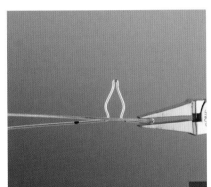

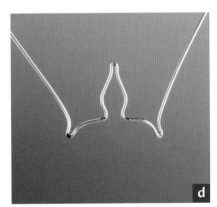

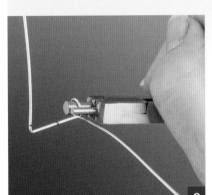

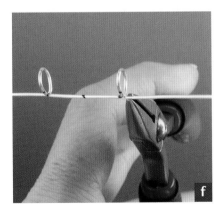

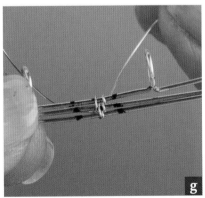

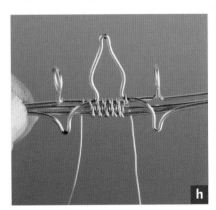

side (the mark shows you where to stop weaving and add the peak) **(photo g)**. Continue with the 2-1 weave until you reach the marks on either side. Add the peak by weaving it to the bail wire **(photo h)**. Continue the weave to the lower peaks, and wrap it to the bottom wire once **(photo i)**. Continue weaving until the weaving wire reaches the bail loops. Wrap the weaving wire around the bail loops once **(photo j)**. Weave about four or five more 2-1 weave pairs, then include the peak wire in the last two rows of weaves **(photo k)**. Cut the weaving wire.

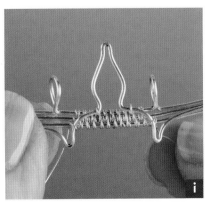

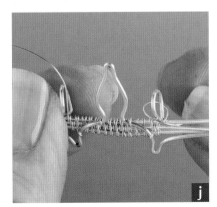

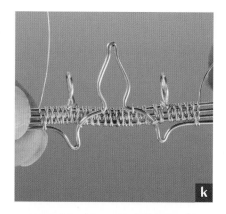

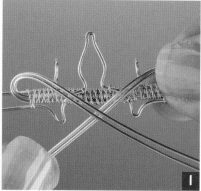

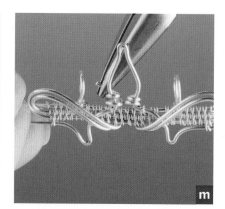

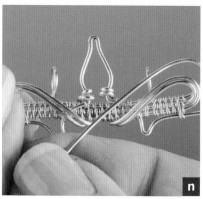

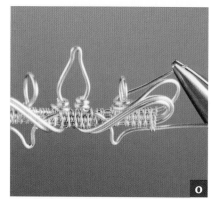

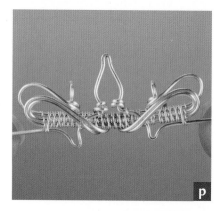

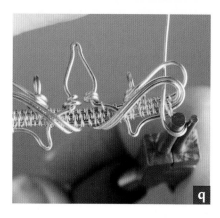

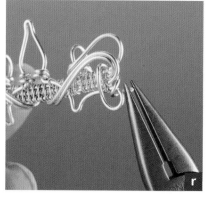

4 / Ornate bail loops

Finger-loop the center two wires inward, on the left and right side, until they cross in the center of the peak; keep the wires parallel (**photo l**). Bring the two pairs of wires behind the weave, in the center, and up to the base of the peak, and wrap each of the four wires once around the peak base (**photo m**). Finger-loop the top right wire inward and downward so it is a little higher than the previous loops (**photo n**).

Wrap it twice around the base of the bail loop (**photo o**). Repeat on the opposite side (**photo p**).

5 / The lower loops

Make an inward and downward loop on the fourth bottom wire with 3mm bail-forming pliers on the left and right side. Bring the ends up through the three loops above it at the end of the weave (**photo q**). Bring the wire up and behind the weave, and coil it one time at the top of the loop just made (**photo r**). Add a 4mm bead to the center of the peak with 10cm 28-gauge wire.

6 / Attach the two secured loops

These secured lower loops will connect the bail to the pendant on the left and right side. Cut two 10cm pieces of 22-gauge wire. Use 3mm bail-forming pliers to make a loop, and slide the loop onto the bail either at the bottom point or the lower bail loop. Secure the loop, add a 3mm metal bead, and create a second loop to attach to the pendant. Secure that loop and cut the wires (**photo s**).

SONORAN SUNRISE PENDANT

The contrasting colors of the Sonoran Sunrise (also called Sonoran Sunset) stone are a naturally occurring color combination within the rock. The stone colors are a meeting of red cuprite and green chrysocolla. I have loved this palette for years, and I have now found it in nature.

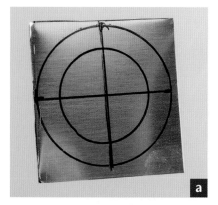

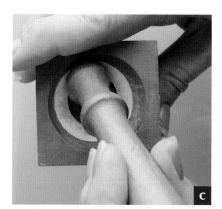

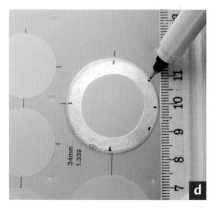

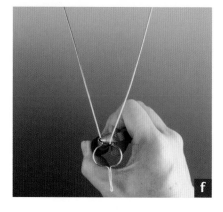

NOTE: This piece will be worked upside down and will be flipped over at the end. Complete each step on the right and left sides of the piece.

1 / Make the washer

Use a 35mm circle template, draw an outer circle onto a 4cm square of 26-gauge sterling silver sheet. Mark on the metal where the circle template quadrant marks are, and then draw a cross connecting those marks. Draw a 22mm inner circle within the outer circle; line up the quadrant lines to keep it centered **(photo a)**. Punch the inner circle out with a disk cutter by lining up the inner circle drawn on the metal with the corresponding hole in the disk cutter **(photo b)**. Punch out the disk (see "Disk Cutting," p. 16).

Cut around the larger outer circle using metal shears. If a metal pattern is desired (see "Patterning Metal with Brass Plates and Texturing with Metal Stamps," p. 18), add it now or you may

risk distorting the circular shape. I chose to stamp the metal with a random pattern. Patterning will work-harden the metal; anneal and pickle the metal Place the ring pattern-side down in a wooden dapping block. Use a wooden dap to form the ring into a convex form (see "Disk Doming," p. 17) **(photo c)**. File the inside and outside edges.

Place the washer into a circle template (with four quadrant marks) closest to the size of the washer. Mark these four points on the washer for a reference for making five holes. Next, make a mark 1cm to the left and to the right from the bottom mark for hole location **(photo d)**. Make the same marks at the top. Punch five holes into the circle: two at the bottom and three at the top. Make sure these five holes are about 1mm from the outside edge of the washer.

2 / Create the bottom disk

Using metal shears, cut a 4cm circle from a 4.5cm square of 28- or 26-gauge

sheet metal. If you want the metal patterned, pattern it first before cutting. I used a craft embossing machine to emboss the metal. You do not need to anneal this piece, as it will remain flat. Center the washer onto the bottom disk, and tape these to a hard surface to stabilize both pieces. Make sure the tape doesn't cover any of the holes in the washers. Using the holes in the washer as a guide, mark the five holes onto the bottom disk about 2mm from the edge **(photo e)**. Punch out the five holes.

NOTE: Use small pieces of scrap wire to temporarily hold the washer and bottom disk together, making sure that the holes in both are aligned. This helps prevent the metal from shifting while wire wrapping.

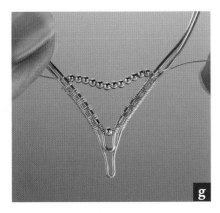

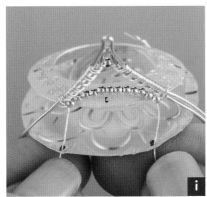

SUPPLIES

o 4cm square 26-gauge dead-soft sterling silver sheet metal

o 4.5cm square 28- or 26-gauge dead-soft sterling silver sheet metal

o 41cm 18-gauge dead-soft round wire

o 120cm 20-gauge dead-soft round wire

o 122cm 22-gauge dead-soft round wire

o 100cm 26-gauge dead-soft round wire

o 540cm 28-gauge dead-soft round wire

o 24–26mm round cabochon with a narrow girdle (edge)

o **13** 2mm metal beads

o **3** 3mm metal beads

o **1** 4mm metal bead

TOOLS

o Wire Toolkit

o Metal shears

o Wooden dap and dapping block

o Permanent marker

o Metal file

o 1.25mm hole punching pliers

o Temporary blue painters tape

o Hammer and steel bench block

o 1.5mm, 3mm, and 5mm bail-forming pliers

o 32mm and 11mm dowels

o 22mm round disk cutter

o 22mm, 35mm, and 45mm circle templates

o Patterning Metal Toolkit (optional)

o Soldering Toolkit (optional)

o Finishing and Polishing Toolkit (optional)

3 / The bail component

Cut a 40cm piece of 20-gauge wire and hard-fold it in half (see "Hard Fold," p. 12). Measure and mark 1.5cm from the fold, and make another mark 2cm from the first mark. Bend both ends outward at the first mark, parallel to the floor and on the same plane. Use an 11mm dowel to form an arch on both sides of the bend, beginning at the first mark and ending at the second mark. Bend the wire up at the second mark **(photo f)**. Hammer the arches gently on a steel bench block to work-harden them. Set the bail component aside.

4 / Weave the frame

Cut 35cm of 18-gauge wire and 40cm of 20-gauge wire. Soft-fold both of these wires in half, and gently spread the ends (see "Soft Fold," p. 12). Cut 350cm of 28-gauge weaving wire, and string a 2mm metal bead to the center. Place the bead inside of the 18-gauge peak, and coil three times on either side of the peak. Line up the peak of the 20-gauge wire below the peak of the 18-gauge wire, and wrap the two wires together three times. Coil three times onto the 20-gauge wire. Continue this 3-3 weave for a total of six pairs on the left and right side of the peaks. String 12 2mm beads onto the right side of the weaving wire. Bring that weaving wire over to the opposite side, and coil one time. Pass back through all the beads with the left side weaving wire, and coil once on the right side **(photo g)**.

5 / Attach the woven frame to the washer and disk

Remove the bottom two scrap wires securing the washer and disk; leave the scrap wires on the three upper holes. Bring the right 28-gauge weaving wire of the frame through the top of the right lower hole in the washer. Wrap around the inner 18-gauge frame wire and then back through the same hole. Wrap around the 18-gauge wire **(photo h)**. Thread the weaving wire down through the disk. Do this on the left and right sides **(photo i)**. Wrap around the outer 20-gauge frame wire and then back through the same hole in the disk, and coil around the 20-gauge frame wire.

TIP: If you don't have a disk cutter, drill a hole in the center and saw out the inner circle.

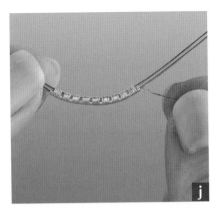

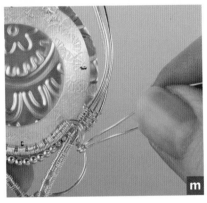

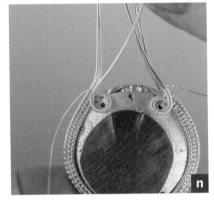

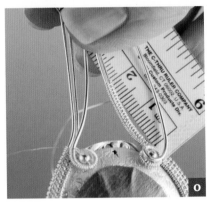

6 / Make the upper trim

This step adds ornamentation to obscure the lower holes. Cut two 15cm pieces of 22-gauge wire. Cut 60cm of 28-gauge weaving wire. Begin the weave at the center of both the 22-gauge wires and the weaving wire. This is a 5-2 weave, which consists of two coils around the lower wire and then five wraps around both wires. Do this weave for a total of nine five-wraps and 10 double-coils. End with two coils on the left and right sides of the lower wire (**photo j**). Secure the trim to the wire frame by coiling the trim weaving wire two times onto the 18-gauge inner frame wire. Trim the weaving wire. Don't cut the 22-gauge wires.

7 / Attach the bail component

Form the point of the bail component into a slight arch so it will lay nicely around the frame. Bring the peak of the bail component under the 2mm bead at the lower wire frame peak. This will help stabilize the bail. Bring the straight bail component wires up and alongside the 18-gauge and the 20-gauge frame wires. At this time, the 18-gauge frame wire is on the inside, the 20-gauge frame wire is in the middle, and the bail component wire is on the outside. Wrap the frame weaving wire around the bail component wire and the outer 20-gauge frame wire twice (**photo k**).

8 / Weave the bail wire and the frame

Using the frame weaving wire, begin a 2-1 weave on the frame wires and the bail component wire (see "2-1 Weave," p. 20). Do not weave the upper trim wires. Begin with a single coil on the outside bail wire, then a single coil on the middle 20-gauge wire, and a single coil on the inner 18-gauge wire. Follow this by wrapping the weaving wire around the inner 18-gauge and the middle 20-gauge, and then wrapping the weaving wire around the 20-gauge and the bail wire. Continue this 2-1 weave for about 1cm (**photo l**).

9 / Secure the upper trim wires to the bail

Arch the upper trim wire pairs downward, and wrap the wire ends around the base of the bail wires once. Trim the excess wire (**photo m**).

10 / Weave the frame wires

Continue weaving the 2-1 weave up to the outer top holes. Insert the cabochon. Tape the cabochon with temporary tape to prevent marring of the stone's surface. Secure the left and right holes of the washer and disk with the weaving wire the same manner as the two lower holes. Leave the center hole open. Coil 1.5cm up the inner 18-gauge wire with the weaving wire. Curve that coiled inner wire down toward the center, and make a full circle around the left and right holes (**photo n**).

NOTE: Follow steps 11 and 12 on both the left and right sides.

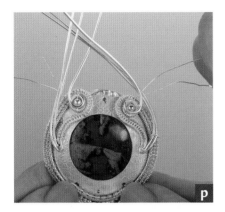

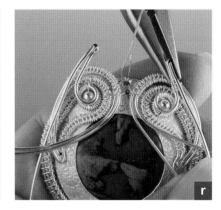

11 / Create the outer ornate leaf pattern

Add a 3mm bead to the weaving wire, and tuck the bead into the center of the coiled circle. Coil once on the other side of the circle, and re-string the weaving wire back through the 3mm bead. Frame the bead by making another circle on top of the coiled circle with the 18-gauge wire. Bring the 18-gauge wire to the top. Continue the 2-1 weave on the middle and outer 20-gauge wire for an additional 2cm **(photo o)**. Bring the 2cm woven middle and outer 20-gauge wires down and around the coiled circle. Arch that weave inward. Mark 5mm from the end of the weave, and create a sort of leaf shape by hard-folding both wires at the mark. Bring the weaving wire across to the other side of the leaf shape, and secure it to the woven frame to offer stability to the shape **(photo p)**. Trim and save the excess weaving wire.

12 / Create the inner leaf pattern

Bring the frame wires to their original parallel position of the 18-gauge on the inside, the 20-gauge in the middle and the other 20-gauge on the outside. Using the remaining weaving wire that was just cut, coil once around the 18-gauge, then once around the 20-gauge and once on the outer 20-gauge wire. Wrap the outer 20-gauge wire to the middle 20-gauge wire. Wrap the middle 20-gauge wire to the 18-gauge inner wire. Pull the 18-gauge wire up, and begin a 2-1 weave with the weaving wire on the two 20-gauge wires. Weave about 1.5cm, and start arching the weave around the inside of the secured leaf shape. Continue to weave until the weave reaches the top hole.

Now, you'll begin the inner leaf shape, which needs stability. Bring the weaving wire over to the large leaf, coil once onto the existing weave, and then return the weaving wire back to the 20-gauge wires. Use a pin to separate the washer from the bottom disk to create a space so the weaving wire can move through the hole easier in the next step **(photo q)**. Catch the weaving wires through

the top hole, wrap the wires around the washer and disk at the edge, and then remove the pin.

Measure 5mm from the weave up the 18-gauge wire. Hard-fold down and out on the mark on the left and right sides **(photo r)**. Open up the fold slightly, bring the free side of the 18-gauge wire to the back of the piece, and bend the two peaks slightly outward **(photo s)**. This creates the pegs.

Hard-fold the two inner 20-gauge wires toward the center and upward to create the two small leaves (about 1cm from the top hole). Wrap the 20-gauge wire ends around the two peaks once. Bring the wire ends to the back **(photo t)**, and cut the excess wire.

NOTE: If your cabochon is smaller than the dimensions of the washer given in this lesson, you can adjust by using smaller outer and inner circles.

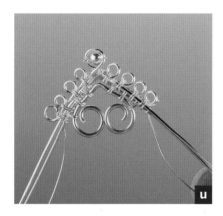

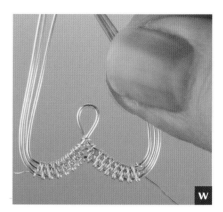

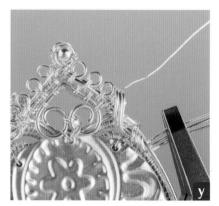

13 / Continuous loop and heart lace

Cut 15cm of 22-gauge wire for the continuous loops. Use 1.5mm bail-forming pliers to create four continuous loops followed by a fifth loop with the 3mm bail-forming pliers, then four more with the 1.5mm bail-forming pliers (see "Continuous Loops," p. 19). Bend the continuous loops so the 3mm top loop makes a sort of peak and the smaller loops slope downward.

Cut 15cm of 22-gauge wire for the lace frame. Soft-fold this wire at its midpoint; place it so it supports the continuous loops. Cut 6cm of 18-gauge wire and create a heart shape (see **photo u**). Cut 70cm of 28-gauge wire for weaving. String a 3mm metal bead to the middle of the weaving wire, and place the bead inside the 3mm peak of the continuous loops. Coil once around the left and right side of the middle loop with the weaving wire. Drop the weaving wire to the peak of the lace frame wire, and coil twice onto the frame wire. Double-wrap around the inside of the next loop to the frame wire. Double-wrap the frame wire to the heart. Double-wrap the next continuous loop to the frame wire. Continue with this double-wrap until all the continuous loops have been wrapped, ending with one coil on the frame wire **(photo u)**.

14 / Attach the continuous loop and heart lace to the pendant

Bring the weaving wires down to the curves at the top of the heart, add a 4mm bead to the center of the heart, and secure the heart to the top hole of the washer with the weaving wires. Bring the weaving wires up and out, and coil them to the left and right pegs. Trim the weaving wires. Bring the excess lace frame wires down and in front of the top of the large leaves. Coil each frame wire one time, and cut the excess lace wires **(photo v)**.

15 / Bead frame and weave swag

Cut 20cm of 22-gauge wire for a loop. Make a teardrop-shaped loop in the center of the wire with 3mm bail-forming pliers. Pull outward on the loop a bit, and check to be sure it will frame the bead in the upper part of the lace.

Cut 50cm of 28-gauge weaving wire. Wrap the center of the weaving wire around the base of the loop one time. Bend 20cm of 22-gauge wire in half at a 90-degree angle for a middle frame wire. Add 20cm of 22-gauge wire for the inner frame wire after bending at a 90-degree angle. Weave 2-1 weave on the left and right side of the frame using all three wires. The weave should be long enough to cover most of the left and right continuous loop woven wires (about 1cm on each side). Arch the weave outward a small amount to create the swag **(photo w)**.

Cut 10cm of 28-gauge wire, string through the 3mm bead in the center of the continuous loop weave, coil on both the frame and the bead wire twice, and then coil once on the frame **(photo x)**. Cut the excess wire. Secure the lower swag by coiling the remaining weaving wires to the continuous loop frame. Cut the weaving wire. Bring the swag wire trios up and over to the back of the piece, and wrap the wires around the

20-gauge wire until the weaving wire reaches the upper 18-gauge wire with the loose wrap **(photo z)**. Do not cut the weaving wire yet. Once the two wires are woven together, arch the 20-gauge wire inward, and then spiral the ends. Use the weaving wire to anchor the spiral by wrapping twice around the spiral and then coiling onto the 20-gauge wire. Cut the weaving wire **(photo aa, back of piece)**. Coil the 18-gauge wire one time on the bail loops near the peak. Cut the 18-gauge wire close to the bail loops, and tighten that coil with chainnose pliers.

Finish by adding patina, if desired.

back of the piece onto the back side of the peg wire. This is somewhat of a loose organic spiral wrapping down the wire **(photo y, back of piece)**. Cut the excess wire, and burnish.

16 / Finish the back

Cut 30cm of 20-gauge wire, and gently bend it in an arch or use a 32mm dowel to shape the wire. Cut 100cm of 26-gauge weaving wire, and begin to coil the middle of the 20-gauge wire with the middle of the 26-gauge weaving wire. Coil to the left and right about 2cm. Place the arched coiled wire onto the bottom of the of the back of the pendant. (The 20-gauge wire ends are facing up, while the 18-gauge wire ends are facing down.) Secure the weaving wire into the bottom holes from the back.

Coil about five coils past the bail loops, and double-wrap the weaving wire around the 20-gauge wire and the 18-gauge peg wire. Continue to coil seven times on the 20-gauge wire, and double-wrap the 18-gauge wire to the

17 / Orient the necklace

Thread the chain through the bail loops and behind the peak, or use a secure loop on either side and attach the bail loops to a chain **(photo bb)**.

design variation
Look for other low-dome cabochon options, like this hand-painted ceramic lotus from Golem Design Studio. Alternately, hang this pendant upside down for added interest.

AROMATHERAPY NECKLACE

This piece is a form of functional jewelry. The necklace not only has an intricately wired frame, but it also provides the wearer with a spherical bead that can be immersed in essential oils, colognes, or perfume. Porous stones, such as lava rock or a crystalized centered rock, work nicely.

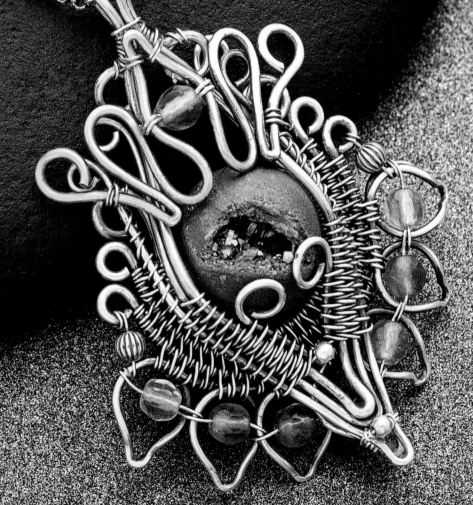

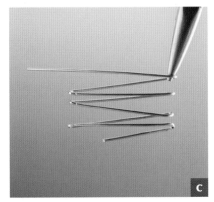

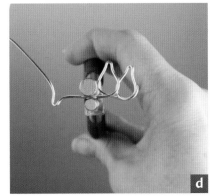

SUPPLIES

- 50.5cm 20-gauge dead-soft round wire
- 50cm 18-gauge dead-soft round wire
- 290cm 28-gauge dead-soft round wire
- 7cm 16-gauge dead-soft round wire
- **1** 12mm aromatherapy bead
- **2** 2mm metal beads
- **2** 3mm metal beads
- **8** 4mm stone beads
- Pipette/eye dropper
- Essential oil

TOOLS

- Wire Toolkit
- 6mm, 3mm, and 1.5mm bail-forming pliers
- 20mm and 13mm dowels/mandrels
- Finishing and Polishing Toolkit (optional)

Make the first leaf-shape: Using 6mm bail-forming pliers, begin the continuous loop technique by rolling wire around the pliers. There will be wire overlap. When you reach the first peak, roll the pliers over that peak. Begin the next leaf-shape by putting the pliers against the previous leaf shape, and roll the wire over the pliers toward the next peak **(photo d)**. All peaks should be facing upward. You may need to finesse the wire during rolling with the pliers to make sure the peaks are all aligned upward **(photo e)**. Continue to make the leaf shapes until you have seven total. Allow a little overlap with the last leaf. Trim the excess wire.

3 / Make the arch bead frame

Cut 7cm of 16-gauge wire. Form the wire around a 13mm dowel to make a curve. Make a basic loop outward on each end of the wire with 3mm bail-forming pliers. Spread the circle a bit to fit the aromatherapy bead. Cut 6cm of 18-gauge wire. Form the wire around a 20mm dowel, and make a basic loop outward at the wire ends using 1.5mm bail-forming pliers. Spread this outward to fit around the half-circle.

2 / Make the leaf-shaped trim

NOTE: This component is challenging, so try making it with copper or other non-precious metal first. The trim is a modification of "Continuous Loops," p. 19. Being familiar with this technique is very helpful for understanding the step. The only difference in the two techniques is that this trim has points that need to be considered while forming the wire around the pliers.

Cut 26cm of 20-gauge wire. To make this trim, it is important to measure your marks precisely. If even one mark is off by as little as 1mm, this will render the trim askew. Make the first mark 2.1mm from the wire end. Make the next mark 3.2mm from the first mark. Make five more marks 3.2mm from the previous mark. So, you will have one mark at 2.1mm and six more marks spaced 3.2mm apart. Hard-fold in at each mark with the chainnose pliers (see "Hard Fold," p. 12) **(photo c)**. Open up all the folds so all the points are facing down.

1 / Charge the bead with oil

Typically, I use essential oils with my aroma beads, but perfumes and other fragrant oils may also be used. Use an eye dropper to place oil onto the bead. How long will the fragrance last? The answer to this varies, depending upon the quality of the essential oil, the properties of the perfume and the type of bead used. Clay beads seems to hold and absorb the oil most effectively. Essential oils are susceptible to aroma deterioration and are best stored in amber bottles to protect them from sunlight **(photos a and b)**.

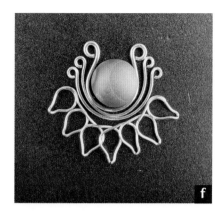

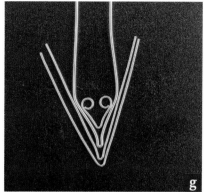

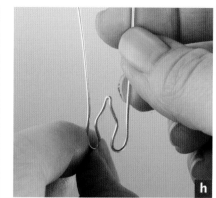

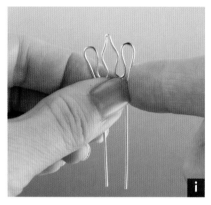

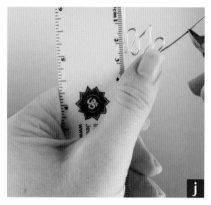

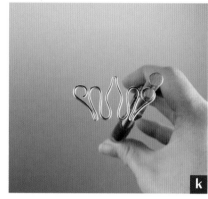

Cut 6cm of 18-gauge wire. Form around a 20mm dowel, and make outward basic loops at the wire ends using 1.5mm bail-forming pliers. Spread this outward to fit around the second wire half-circle. Gently arch the leaf-shape trim to match this curve, being careful not to distort the trim; the points should face outward (photo f).

4 / Make the arabesque frame

Cut 20cm of 18-gauge wire. Hard-fold the wire in half. Open the folded wire and form an arabesque shape (see "Arabesque Wire Shape," p. 12) around a 13mm dowel. Cut 10cm of 20-gauge wire. Bend in half at an angle. Cut 10cm of 20-gauge wire. Bend in half at an angle. Cut 4.5cm of 20-gauge wire. Bend at the center of the wire, and turn the wire ends inward with 3mm bail-forming pliers to form a heart. Nest the wires in the image shown for the weaving order of this frame (photo g).

5 / Make the crown

Cut 18cm of 18-gauge wire. Hard-fold the wire in half, and open the fold. Using a 6mm mandrel or bail-forming pliers, create an arabesque shape. Using only your fingers, arch the wires upward evenly at the base of the arabesque shape, and pinch slightly to make a lower wave (photo h). Bring the wires downward, about 1cm, from the last arch, to make an upper wave (photo i). The arch should be lower than the peak. Hard-fold the wires upward with pliers so the fold is about 2mm above the lower wave. Measure 2.5cm from the hard fold, and flush-cut the wire (photo j). Create an inward loop on each side using 3mm-forming bail pliers (photo k).

6 / Weave the arch bead frame

Cut 140cm of 28-gauge weaving wire, and mark at the halfway point. Starting at the midpoint of the weaving wire, begin a 2-1 weave (see "2-1 Weave," p. 12) at the center petal of the leaf-shaped trim and the midpoint of the

outer half circle of the arch bead frame. Wrap once around the center petal and the outer half-circle. Wrap once around the outer half-circle and the middle half-circle. Wrap once around the middle half-circle and the inner half-circle. Coil once on the inner half-circle. Coil once on the middle half-circle. Coil once on the outer half-circle (photo l). Coil once on the center petal. Continue with 2-1 weave on the left and right side to about 5mm from the loop on the inner half-circle. There will be one or two lines of the weave between each leaf shape. Decrease the weave close to the top. Cut the weaving wire.

7 / Weave the bail

Cut 70cm of 28-gauge weaving wire, and mark the midpoint. String a 2mm metal bead on the weaving wire and place it on the mark. Place the 2mm bead inside the peak of the heart, and start the downslope weave by wrapping the weaving wire around the heart and the inner arabesque wire, then wrapping the inner frame wire to the middle

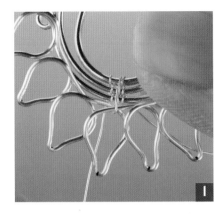
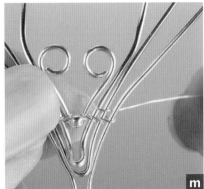
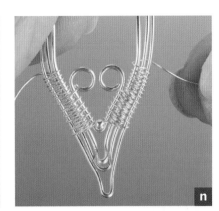

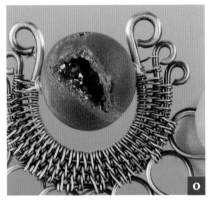
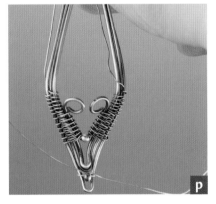
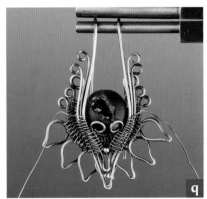

frame wire, and finally wrapping the middle frame wire to the outer frame wire. Continue this double-wrap on the upslope (**photo m**). Continue this weave to the top of the arches of the heart (the arches are not included in the weave). Leave a 15cm tail with the weaving wire (**photo n**).

8 / Add a patina

Apply a patina now, if desired, so the aromatherapy bead doesn't absorb the liver of sulfur. Patinate the arch bead frame with the leaf-shaped trim, the arabesque frame, the crown, two 3mm beads, one 2mm bead, and 80cm of 28-gauge wire.

9 / Attach the aromatherapy bead

Cut 15cm of 28-gauge weaving wire, and string the aromatherapy bead. Leaving equal parts of wire on either side of the bead, coil onto the inner half-circle bead frame wire. You may need a straight pin to split the weave and make

room for the coils. Run the 28-gauge wires back through the bead on either side to add strength to the connection. Coil on the weave wire next to the bead to stabilize the bead (**photo o**).

10 / Attach the frames and form the bail

Arch the peaks of the arabesque frame slightly upward with chainnose pliers. Cut 10cm of 28-gauge wire and add a 2mm metal bead to its midpoint. Place the bead in the lower peak of the arabesque frame, and coil once on either side of the peak (**photo p**). Lay the arabesque frame on top of the arch bead frame so the lower peak of the arabesque frame lines up with the middle leaf-shape at the bottom of the arch frame. Using the 28-gauge wire attached to the peak of the arabesque frame to coil around both the left and right sides of these peaks to secure them together. Coil the 28-gauge wire beside the 2mm bead to secure the bead (see "Secured Basic Loop," p. 13). Using 1.5mm bail-forming pliers, make small outward

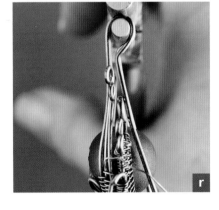

loops onto the middle and outer frame wires of the arabesque frame. Mark 1cm on the inner arabesque frame wire up from the top loop. Place 3mm bail-forming pliers at the mark, and form the wires to the back of the pendant for a bail (**photo q**).

11 / Complete the bail

Leaving the 3mm-forming bail pliers in the formed bail, push the wire ends in toward the piece, creating a more closed loop. Turn the bail wires out at a 90-degree angle (**photo r**), and mark

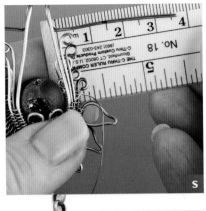

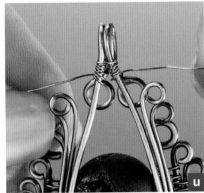

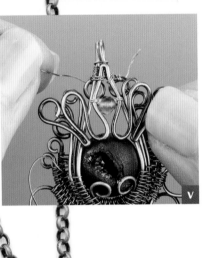

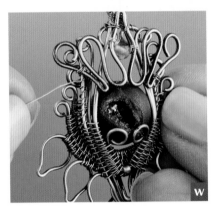

design variation
*Clay beads and copper give the piece
a more rustic and earthy feel.*

them 1.5cm down from the bail **(photo
s)**. Flush-cut the wires on the mark.
Using 3mm bail-forming pliers, turn
the ends of the bail wire in toward the
center and parallel to the pendant
(photo t).

12 / Attach the crown to the bail
Cut 10cm of 28-gauge wire. String a
4mm stone bead onto the middle of the
wire. Secure the bead with two coils
inside the center peak of the crown. Cut
the excess wire. Cut 15cm of 28-gauge
weaving wire and, starting in the middle
of the wire, wrap the weaving wire
around the base of the bail wires, followed by coiling the weaving wire four
or five time onto the bail wires on the
left and right sides **(photo u)**.

Place the crown peak in front of the
base of the bail. Wrap the weaving
wires from the bail around both the bail
wires and the crown peak wires on the
left and right side. Wrap around both
of these wires twice, and coil the wire
ends onto the loops at the top of the

bail wires **(photo v)**. With the remaining weaving wires, coil loosely upward
on the outside arabesque frame wire,
leaving spaces between the coils. Wrap
around the crown ends three times, and
then coil back onto the frame once or
twice **(photo w)**. Cut the wire ends.

13 / Add beads to the trim
Cut 25cm of 28-gauge wire and, leaving
a 2cm tail, coil twice onto the left outer
leaf shape on the leaf trim. Bring the
wire across the leaf shape, string a 4mm
stone bead, and coil on top and around
the first and second leaf shape where
the wires meet. String a second bead,
and coil around where the second and
third leaf shapes intersect. Continue
adding the remaining beads. Coil two
times on the end of the final leaf. Add a
3mm bead to both ends of the 28-gauge
wire, and coil onto the loop above the
first and last leaf shape. Turn the tips
of the leaf-shapes back slightly with
bail-forming or chainnose pliers **(photo
x)**. Spread the bail loops apart slightly.

OCEAN'S TREASURE EARRINGS

These elegant earrings have a soldered peg to secure a half-drilled pearl. The techniques outlined in this project include soldering, attaching a half-drilled pearl, and finger-bending wire. When choosing pearls, consider color, size, consistent luster, and shape.

SUPPLIES

- o 6cm 12-gauge dead-soft sterling silver square wire
- o 22cm 16-gauge fine-silver round wire
- o 28cm 18-gauge fine-silver round wire
- o 34cm 20-gauge fine-silver round wire
- o 200cm 28-gauge dead-soft fine-silver round wire
- o **2** 6mm half-drilled pearls
- o **2** 3mm metal round beads
- o Pair of earring wires

TOOLS

- o Soldering Toolkit
- o Wire Toolkit
- o 9mm dowel/mandrel
- o Metal pattern stamp
- o Steel bench block
- o Chasing hammer
- o Metal file
- o Progressively finer sanding blocks
- o Drill press or flexshaft and #65 drill bit
- o Protective glasses and facemask
- o Pearl vise
- o Two-part epoxy
- o Patina (optional)
- o Toothpicks

NOTE: These earrings are mirror images of each other. While the steps are the same for each earring, mirror the second earring.

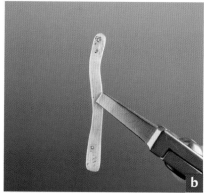
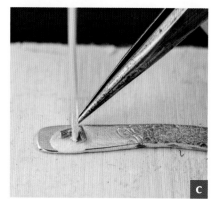
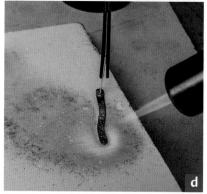
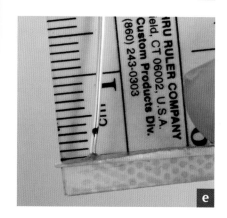
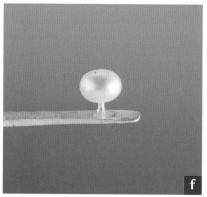

1 / Drill the pearl

This project requires that the pearl sit upon a 20-gauge wire, so drill your pearl if needed (see "Enlarging a Pearl Hole," p. 18). You will only drill halfway into the pearl with a #65 drill bit **(photo a)**.

2 / Create the earring base

Cut 3cm of 12-gauge square wire, and shape it into a slight "S" curve. Hammer the wire flat with a chasing hammer on a bench block, making the bottom a little larger than the top. Make sure the earring base is 38mm long. Anneal and pickle the metal (see "Annealing,"

p. 12). Stamp a random pattern on the top of the wire with a metal stamp (see "Texturing Metal with Stamps," p. 18). Leave the larger portion unstamped about 12mm from the bottom. File the ends round, and file and sand the edges smooth. Drill a hole 1.5cm from the thinner end and a second hole 5mm from the thinner end (see "Drilling with a Drill Press," p. 18) **(photo b)**. Drill a third hole 5mm from the wide end.

3 / Solder the pearl to the base

Cut 3cm of 20-gauge wire. Insert the 20-gauge wire into the hole in

the wide end while on a firebrick or Solderite board. Hold the wire peg with cross-locking tweezers in a third hand. Flux the wire and the base, and put two small pallions of easy-solder wire at the base of the peg **(photo c)**. Using a butane torch, heat the base farthest from the peg and slowly move in with the flame toward the peg until the solder flows **(photo d)**. Quench and pickle. This is a delicate mission, as the wire peg can melt much quicker than the earring base, so heat up the base first.

54

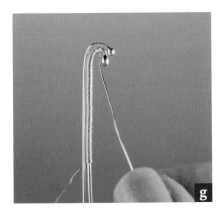

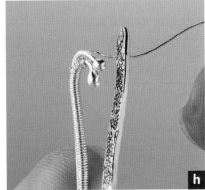

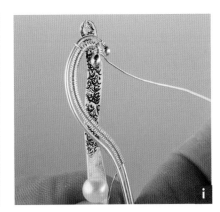

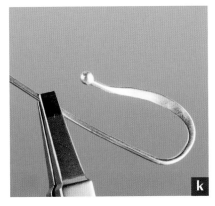

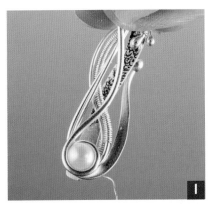

4 / Attach the pearl to the peg

Sand the back side of the base. To measure how long the peg should be, insert the half-drilled pearl onto a 20-gauge wire, and make a mark at the bottom of the pearl where the pearl stops on the wire. Remove the pearl from the wire and measure the mark to the end of the wire. Add 1mm to that measurement. Transcribe the measurement, plus the 1mm up the peg from the earring base, and make a mark **(photo e)**. Flush-cut the peg wire at that mark, and roughen the peg a little with a file. (Do not file so vigorously that you change the peg diameter.) Mix two-part epoxy and apply a drop to the top of the peg. Insert the pearl onto the epoxied peg **(photo f)**. Some excess epoxy is desirable and will be covered up in subsequent steps. Let the epoxy dry for eight hours.

5 / Wire coils and loops

Cut 11cm of 16-gauge wire, 14cm of 18-gauge wire, and 14cm of 20-gauge wire. Torch-bead one end of each wire (see "Torch-Beading a Wire End," p.

12). The measurements will be different; now, they are 10.5cm of 16-gauge, 13.5cm of 18-gauge, and 13.5cm of 20-gauge. Form a tight arch on the beaded end of the 18-gauge wire. Arch the 20-gauge wire so that it follows on top of and along the 18-gauge wire. Cut 100cm of 28-gauge weaving wire. Leaving a 20cm tail, coil the weaving wire six time onto the arch of the 18-gauge wire at the beaded end. Wrap the weaving wire around both the 18-gauge and the 20-gauge wires once, and then continue to coil on the 18-gauge wire for 2.5cm **(photo g)**. Insert the weaving wire into the lower hole in the top narrow end of the earring base. Bring that wire around the side of the base. Coil twice around the 20-gauge wire, and then coil twice around the 18-gauge wire. Don't cut the wire end **(photo h)**. Create an "S" shape with the two wires. Coil onto the 20-gauge wire until the coil reaches the pearl **(photo i)**. Wrap both the wires around the bottom of the pearl, and cross the wires over and across themselves **(photo j)**.

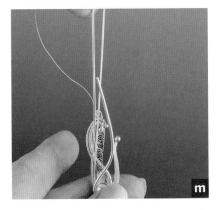

6 / Create a fish-hook wire arch

Make a fish-hook arch with the 16-gauge wire on a 9mm mandrel about 2.5cm from the beaded end wire. Vigorously hammer the side of the wire under the beaded end and about a third of the arch. Sand this wire smooth **(photo k)**. Hook this arch around the bottom of the pearl, and form the 16-gauge wire tighter around the pearl, framing the pearl and trailing that wire end upward **(photo l)**.

7 / Make more curves and loops

Wrap the 18-gauge wire **(photo m)**

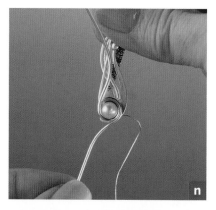

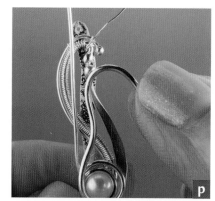

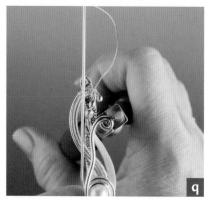

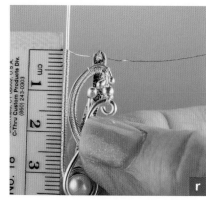

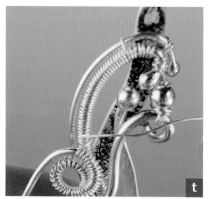

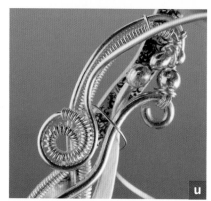

around the top and side of the pearl **(photo n)**, and make a small loop just below the pearl with roundnose pliers **(photo o)**. Using fingers, make a double wave with the 16-gauge wire **(photo p)**. Cut the wire even with the top of the earring base, and make an outward loop with the end **(photo q)**. Using the weaving wire at the top of the base, string a 3mm metal bead, coil onto the 16-gauge loop twice, string back through the bead, and coil onto the 18-gauge wire.

8 / Coil the 20-gauge wire

Coil 3cm onto the straight 20-gauge wire to the left of the earring with the remaining weaving wire **(photo r)**. Finger-bend the top of the coiled portion of the wire in an outward spiral **(photo s)**. Secure the loop with the weaving wire to the 18-gauge wire **(photo t)**. Spiral the 20-gauge wire upon itself once more **(photo u)**. Make an inward-facing loop above the spiral with the 20-gauge wire, and trim the excess wire **(photo v)**. Secure that loop by coiling upon it twice with the 28-gauge weaving wire **(photo w)**. Attach an earring wire, and apply patina, if desired. Repeat to make a second earring.

ASTRAEA EARRINGS

Astraea is known as the Greek goddess of justice and innocence. The name is associated with the sign Virgo, and the name is derived from the Greek meaning of "star" (aster). These earrings hold the shape of a goddess and the circles of the celestial.

SUPPLIES

- o 12cm 16-gauge dead-soft square wire
- o 34cm 16-gauge dead-soft round wire
- o 16cm 18-gauge dead-soft round wire
- o 30cm 26-gauge dead-soft round wire
- o 260cm 28-gauge dead-soft round wire
- o **2** 10x6mm briolettes or pear-shaped gemstones
- o **2** 7x5mm briolettes or teardrop-shaped gemstones
- o **2** 3mm soldered jump rings
- o **2** 3mm gemstone beads
- o **4** 2mm metal beads
- o Pair of earring wires

TOOLS

- o Wire Toolkit
- o Torch Toolkit
- o Steel bench block
- o Chasing hammer
- o 9mm and 12mm dowels or mandrels
- o 3mm dowel or bail-making pliers

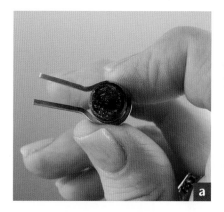

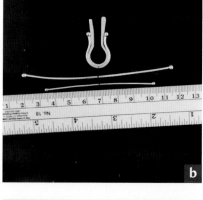

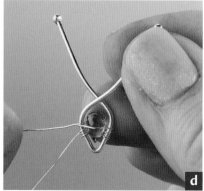

1 / Make the frame

Cut 6cm of 16-gauge square wire and mark the middle of the wire. Form the wire around a 9mm dowel. Bend the ends up slightly **(photo a)**. Hammer the ends of the wire to flatten them. File and sand the edges and hammered sections until smooth. Cut 6cm of round 16-gauge wire, and torch-bead both ends of the wire (see "Torch-Beading a Wire End," p. 12); the new length should be 52mm. Wrap the round 16-gauge wire ¾ of the way around a 12mm mandrel, making sure the beaded ends are evenly aligned. Fit the round 16-gauge wire around the square 16-gauge wire with both ends pointing upward.

Cut 11cm of 16-gauge round wire, torch-bead the ends (torched length is 9.5cm), and mark the middle of that wire. Cut 8cm 18-gauge round wire, torch-bead the ends (torched length is about 7cm), and mark the middle of that wire **(photo b)**. Soft-fold the 18-gauge wire at the mark (see "Soft Fold," p. 12); open it and form the wire around roundnose pliers

(see "Arabesque Wire Shape," p. 12). Make sure the opening of this shape will fit a 7x5mm briolette. Cross the wires at the top of the shape **(photo c)**.

2 / Make a teardrop briolette frame wire

Cut 30cm of 28-gauge weaving wire and thread a 7x5mm briolette to the middle of the wire. Turn the briolette upside down, and place it into the small arabesque frame. Coil three times to the left and right of the bottom of the frame. Bring the right wire across the front of the briolette and coil onto the left side of the frame **(photo d)**. Bring the left wire across the back of the briolette, and coil once on the right side of the frame. Bring the right wire across the front of the briolette and coil once; bring the left wire around the back of the briolette and coil once. This wire cage offers support to the briolette. You should have a wire to the left and to the right of the frame **(photo e)**. Coil six more times on the left and right of the frame, and trim the weaving wire.

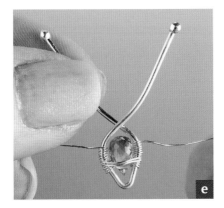
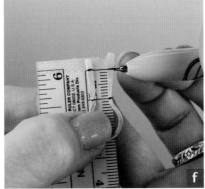
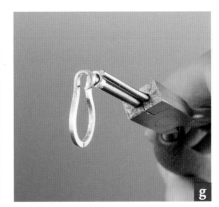

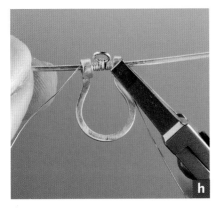
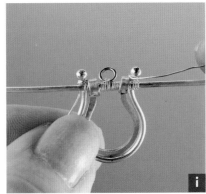
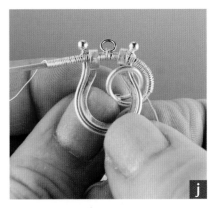

3 / Create a square-wire bail

On the 16-gauge square wire, mark 1.4cm from the midpoint on both sides of the wire. Measure 1cm from the 1.4cm mark, and mark on both sides of the wire **(photo f)**. Flush-cut the ends at the top (1cm) marks. Using 3mm bail-forming pliers, roll each end toward the back to create the bails, but do not make a closed loop **(photo g)**.

4 / Make the frame

Cut 60cm of 28-gauge weaving wire, and coil five times to the left of the middle mark on the 16-gauge round wire. Wrap a soldered jump ring to the middle of the 16-gauge wire with three wraps, and coil five more times to the right of the jump ring. String the square-wire bail on the 16-gauge wire on either side of the coils, and thread the weaving wire through the loops to the outside. Pinch the bails closed with flatnose pliers **(photo h)**. Coil two more times around the round wire. Fit the 16-gauge round wire frame underneath the square-wire bail; the beaded ends should be above

the straight 16-gauge wire to the left and right of the bail. Encircle the weaving wire around the beaded ends of the 18-gauge wire twice **(photo i)**. Continue to coil on the 16-gauge wire for 1cm on the left and right sides.

5 / Loop the wires around the frame

Loop the 16-gauge round wire behind, then in front of the frame wires and between the coil and the frames and toward the back **(photo j)**. Continue to arch the wire until the free beaded ends are in the center of the frame **(photo k)**. Do not cut the weaving wires.

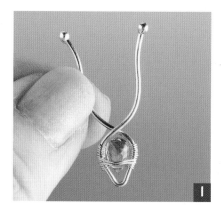
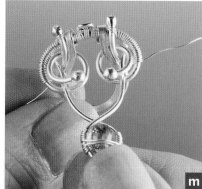

6 / Attach the teardrop briolette frame to the main frame

Slightly spread the teardrop briolette frame ends to the left and right (photo l). Slightly open up the side loops from the front near the beaded ends. Insert the teardrop briolette frame wires under the beaded loop arch and through the loop to the back. You want a small gap between the crossed briolette frame wire and the main frame to allow room for a 3mm bead (photo m, back of the earring). Pull the beaded ends of the briolette frame toward the front, and bend them inward very slightly (photo n, front of the earring). Add a 2mm bead to the weaving wire, and wrap the weaving wire around the beaded end of the teardrop briolette frame wire (photo o). Cut the weaving wire.

7 / Coil the teardrop briolette frame

Cut 40cm of 28-gauge weaving wire, and string a 3mm round stone bead to the middle of the wire. Rest the 3mm bead just above the crossed wires above the teardrop briolette frame. Coil the weaving wire up the wires of the briolette frame until you reach the 16-gauge beaded ends in the middle of the frame. Then, coil the weaving wire to the 16-gauge wire ends (photo p).

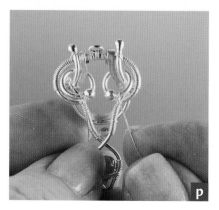

8 / Attach the pear-shaped briolette

Cut 15cm of 26-gauge wire. Attach the 10x6mm pear-shaped briolette to the front of the earring onto the middle loops. Coil twice to the left and right of the bead, and then secure the bead (see "Secured Bead," p. 13).

9 / Finish the earrings

Attach an earring wire loop to the jump ring at the top of the earring. Repeat to make a second earring.

TAXIDERMY EYE PENDANT

The life-like bobcat taxidermy glass eye is the focal point of this pendant. The setting for this piece can alternatively be used for an 18mm round cabochon. Since this particular taxidermy eye is solid, it can be used in this setting. A hollow convex taxidermy eye can be used as well, if you fill it with epoxy resin.

SUPPLIES

- o 30cm 16-gauge round wire
- o 66cm 20-gauge round wire
- o 135cm 22-gauge round wire in a contrasting color
- o 255cm 26-gauge round wire
- o 195cm 28-gauge round wire
- o 4mm stone bead
- o 4mm metal bead
- o **3** 3mm beads
- o **2** 3mm metal spacer beads
- o **4** 2mm metal beads
- o 18mm solid taxidermy eye
- o 15cm necklace chain with links large enough to accept 22-gauge wire

TOOLS

- o Wire Toolkit
- o Temporary blue painters tape
- o 4mm, 11mm, and 16mm dowels
- o 2mm, 3mm, and 4mm bail-forming pliers
- o Permanent marker

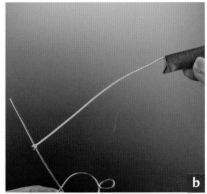

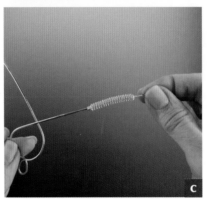

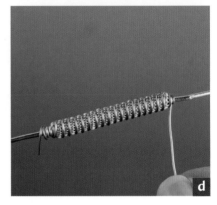

1 / Create the frame

Cut 30cm of 16-gauge wire, and mark in the middle. Make a teardrop loop with 4mm bail-forming pliers at the mark, and cross the wires about 9mm above the pliers. Form the wire around the taxidermy eye until the ends overlap **(photo a)**.

2 / Create double coils

Cut 120cm of 26-gauge weaving wire. Cut 22cm of 20-gauge wire, and coil the weaving wire onto it. The coil should be about 14cm long. Slide the coil to the middle of the 20-gauge wire. There should be equal amounts of 20-gauge uncoiled wire on either side of the coil. Coil the uncoiled end of the 20-gauge wire onto the 16-gauge frame twice. Place a piece of blue painters tape over the other end of the coil and 20-gauge

wire. This tape keeps the coiled coil from sliding around when working **(photo b)**. Continue to coil the coil onto the frame, making sure the wraps are close together **(photo c)**. The coiled coil should be 3.5cm long. Cut 35cm of contrasting-color 22-gauge wire, coil once at the base of the coil, and then wrap around the coiled coil on top of and in-between coils. Do not push the contrasting wire into the spaces of the coiled coil. Coil the contrasting wire onto the other side of the double coil one time **(photo d)**. Cut the 20-gauge and 22-gauge wire ends. Slide the coil down to the frame circle. The circle may distort a little; reshape it around the mandrel. Repeat the coiled-coil on the other side of the frame circle. Bend the frame wire ends up and parallel for the bail **(photo e)**.

3 / Make the twisted circle

Cut 50cm of 22-gauge wire, and make a hard fold at the middle (see "Hard Fold," p. 12). Mark the center of that folded wire. Mark 3cm to the left and 3cm to the right of that mark. Put a thin piece of tape just outside the left and right 3cm marks. Grasp the taped areas with two flatnose pliers, and twist the pliers in opposite directions **(photo f)**. Don't twist too tightly; look for a regular twist pattern. Remove the tape and shape the twisted section on a 16mm dowel. Bend the untwisted wires up and parallel to each other. Cut the original fold at one end.

4 / Hammer the twisted circle

Using a planishing hammer and a bench block, lightly hammer the twisted circle, allowing the twist to flatten and open. It is important that the bottom center of the twisted circle open just enough to allow a 28-gauge wire to pass through it three times. Check the fit of the twisted circle to make sure it will fit nicely inside the double-coiled circle

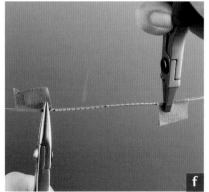

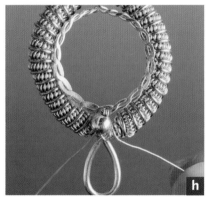

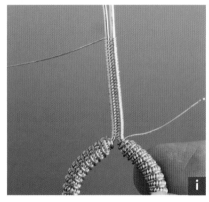

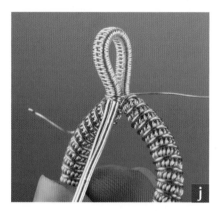

frame. Cut 15cm of 28-gauge weaving wire. Start at the middle of the wire, and coil two or three times around the center bottom twist **(photo g)**. Trail the 28-gauge wire ends downward and together.

5 / Attach the twisted circle to the frame

String a 4mm metal bead on both of the 28-gauge wires, and push the bead up to the base of the twisted circle. Spread the wires apart, and coil each onto the 16-gauge frame twice to the left and right of the bead **(photo h)**.

6 / Weave the bail

Cut 80cm of 28-gauge weaving wire. Leave a 1cm tail, and wrap the end of the wire around the right side of the bail wire twice. Wrap once around both bail wires. Coil once on the left bail wire and then once on the right bail wire. Continue this sequence (wrap-coil-coil-wrap) in a 2-1 weave (see "2-1 Weave," p. 20) for a total of 2.5cm **(photo i)**. Don't cut the weaving wire.

7 / Create the bail

Arch the woven bail toward the back around a 4mm dowel. Bend the un-woven wires outward to create the bail base. Wrap the weaving wire around the base of the bail twice **(photo j)**. String a 3mm bead on the weaving wire, and coil the bead onto the front of the bail and the two twisted circle wire ends at the base. (You are now wrapping the bail wires and the twisted wire ends into a bundle and including that 3mm bead.) Continue to wrap the weaving wire around all the wires and re-insert the weaving wire down through the bead to stabilize the bead **(photo k)**.

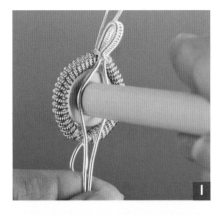

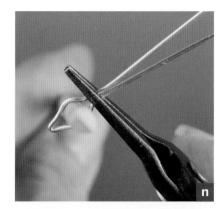

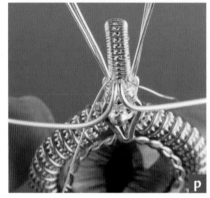

8 / Secure the taxidermy eye

Insert the taxidermy eye behind the coiled coils and twisted circle, and in front of the back (bail) wires. Spread the back wires apart and insert an 11mm dowel against the back of the eye. Pinch the wires under the dowel to create an arabesque shape with the wire ends pointing toward the teardrop loop **(photo l)**. Insert the back wire ends into the teardrop loop from behind, "and coil the back wires twice around the top of the top loop on the left and right sides **(photo m)**. Cut the wire ends close to the coil.

9 / Make the upper arabesque

Cut 22cm of 20-gauge wire, and hard-fold at the middle (see "Hard Fold," p. 12). Open the fold, and shape the wire around a 4mm dowel or bail-forming pliers to make an arabesque shape (see "Arabesque Wire Shape," p. 12) **(photo n)**. Cut 100cm of 28-gauge weaving wire, and string a 3mm bead to the center. Coil the wire twice on the left and right side above the arabesque

shape, with the 3mm bead resting in the middle of the arabesque. Secure the arabesque to the left and right twisted wire ends by coiling three times, making sure the wire ends are pointing upward **(photo o)**. Arch the arabesque wires forward and out to the sides **(photo p)**. Bring the wires to the front of the eye and double coils, and arch them out, then inward toward the bottom loop to create a subtle "S" wave **(photo q)**. Make an outward-facing 3mm loop with bail-forming pliers 5mm from the teardrop loop on the left and right sides **(photo r)**. Then, make a 2mm loop below the first loop with the 2mm bail pliers **(photo s)**. Coil the ends of the wires below the two coils on the teardrop loop.

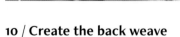

10 / Create the back weave

With the remaining weaving wires from the arabesque loop, make a 2-1 weave on the left and right 22-gauge twisted wire ends **(photo t)**. Bend both weaves to the back and continue that weave until you reach the top of the teardrop loop, forming the weave along the outside of the 16-gauge back wires. Coil the wire ends twice on the left and right side of the loop below the other coils **(photos u and v, back and front of piece)**. Cut the wire ends.

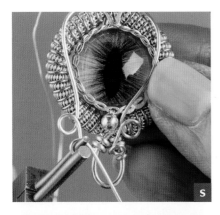

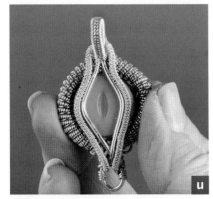

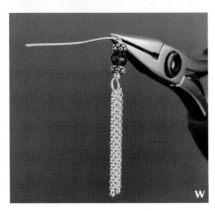

11 / Make the tassel

(See "Briolette Wrap and Dangle," p. 14.) Cut 15cm of 22-gauge wire, and make a 3mm loop 5cm from one end. Attach the end links of five 3mm pieces of chain to the loop. Secure the loop with two or three coils. String a 3mm spacer bead, a 4mm bead, and a spacer bead, and create another 3mm loop above the bead **(photo w)**. Attach this loop to the bottom loop of the eye pendant, and coil to make a secure loop **(photo x)**.

12 / Optional beads at the top

Cut 15cm of 26-gauge wire, and thread through the upper arch. String a 3mm and two 2mm beads on the right wire, and secure the wire end to the back of the frame with three coils. Repeat to add beads to the left side. Patinate the entire piece in liver of sulfur and remove the patina from high points, if desired. (The eye is glass and will repel the liver of sulfur.)

design variation

Reverse your mixed metals from copper on silver to silver on copper. Use a cabochon instead of a taxidermy eye for an entirely different look.

FREE SPIRIT CUFF

This cuff involves exercises in metal stamping, wiring metal, and riveting metal to leather. All of these techniques can be used on a variety of other projects. Choose a different name to stamp, or simply pattern the top metal piece instead.

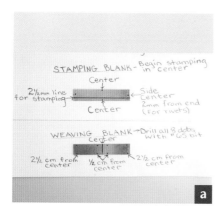

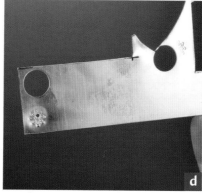

NOTE: The instructions for weaving will complete one quarter of the finished cuff. The top and bottom and the left and the right are mirror images of each other with the same weave.

1 / Stamp the top metal blank

Set one 55x10mm 26-gauge rectangle aside; this is the bottom metal blank. Mark the top and bottom edges at the center of the second rectangle; this mark is the beginning stamp location on the metal. Make a mark on the left and right ends at the center 2mm from the edge; this is the location of the rivet holes. Make a horizontal line across the blank about 3mm up from the bottom edge **(photo a)**. Write out the desired phrase on a piece of paper, and mark the center letter **(photo b)**. First stamp left to right, starting at that center mark, including spaces as a letter space, and then stamp right to left. Stamp each letter 2mm from the edge of the previous letter **(photo c)**. (See "Stamping Words on Metal," p. 17.)

2 / Make the bottom weaving blank

Mark the top and bottom middle of the remaining rectangle blank. Mark 5mm from the middle mark on the left and right and top and bottom. Mark 2.5cm out from the center mark on the left and right and top and bottom. Drill holes at all eight marks with a #65 drill bit (see "Drilling Metal with a Drill Press," p. 16).

3 / Prepare the disks for riveting

These disks stabilize the rivets on the inside of the cuff. Create all the components now so you can rivet after weaving the metal. First, trace around a 9mm disk cutter punch or circle template to draw two circles on a 2.5x2.5cm piece of 26-gauge sheet metal. Stamp a design into the center of the circle, such as a flower (this is optional). Mark the middle of the circle, and use a centering punch to create a divot at the center of the circle. Drill a hole with a #54 drill bit at the center of each circle **(photo d)**. Next, line up the circles drawn on the metals in the 9mm hole in the disk cutter, and use the 9mm punch to punch out each disk **(photo e)** (see "Disk Cutting," p. 16). Set these two disks aside **(photo f)**.

4 / Make a measuring tool

This tool will be used to gauge how long to cut the riveting wire for the rivets. Cut two 2x3cm 26-gauge copper rectangles, align the edges flush, and tape the rectangles together. Set this tool aside for now.

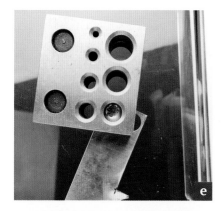

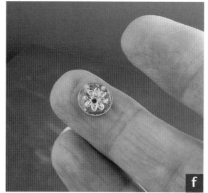

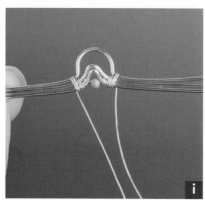

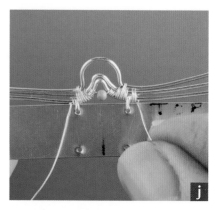

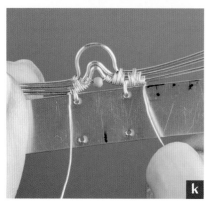

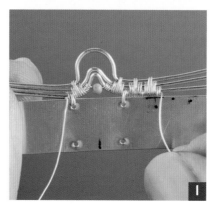

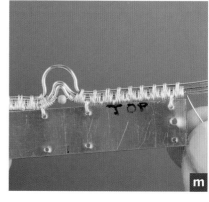

5 / Rivet holes

Tape the stamped rectangle blank on top of the weaving rectangle blank with blue painters tape, making sure all edges are aligned. (Taping these blanks together allows the drill to pierce both metals at the same time and keeps the holes aligned.) Drill two rivet holes on either end of the blanks at the centered end marks of the stamped blank with a #54 drill bit **(photo g)**. Mark one side of the weaving blank "TOP" **(photo h)**.

6 / Weave the top right of the weaving blank

Remember, these weaving instructions are mirror images of the bottom and the top left. Prepare the top and the bottom frames for weaving by cutting six 20cm pieces of 20-gauge wire. Mark all these wires in the middle.

Wire 1: Hard-fold the first 20-gauge wire in the middle (see "Hard Fold," p. 12). Open the fold and pull outward.

Wire 2: Soft-fold the second 20-gauge wire in the middle (see "Soft Fold," p. 12).

Wire 3: Create a centered half-loop with 5mm bail-forming pliers on the third wire. Bend the wires to the left and right

on either side of the half loop. This set of three wires form the top frame wires. Repeat for the set of bottom frame wires.

7 / Make the mountain weave

Cut 210cm of 28-gauge weaving wire, and string a 2mm stone bead to the center of the wire. Place the 2mm bead inside the peak, and coil three times to the left and then the right peak on wire 1. Double-wrap around wires 1 and 2. Double-wrap around all three wires **(photo i)**. Note that all wrapping begins below the frame wires under wire 1. Double-wrap around wires 1 and 2, and

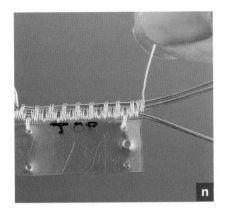

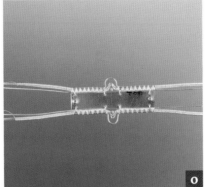

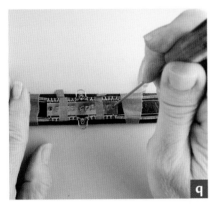

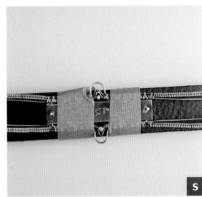

insert the weaving wire end into the first hole of the unstamped weaving blank. Wrap wire 1 to the first hole twice. Double-wrap wire around wires 1 and 2 (photo j). Double-wrap all three wires. Double-wrap wires 1 and 2 (photo k). Here begins the true sequence of this wrap: Coil twice on wire 1. Double-wrap wires 1 and 2. Double-wrap all three wires. Double-wrap wires 1 and 2. Coil twice on wire 1 (photo l). Notice how this wrapping sequence makes a small mountain, and that all wraps and coils begin under wire 1. Repeat this sequence across the frame wires until the weaving wire reaches the second drilled hole in the blank. Double-wrap the hole to wire 1, followed by double-wrapping wire 1 and 2. The weaving wire should be at the end of the metal. If it is not, add another sequence (photo m).

8 / Make the 2-1 weave

Pull wire 1 down and away from wires 2 and 3. Wires 2 and 3 will be woven with the 2-1 weave (see "2-1 Weave," p. 20). Wrap the weaving wire around wires

1 and 2 once. Bring the weaving wire between the wires, and coil once on the wire 3. Bring the wire down behind both wires and up and over wire 2 in a coil. Wrap both wires (photo n), and continue the 2-1 weave for 3.5cm (photo o). Don't cut the weaving wire.

9 / Add patina

If the cuff is to have a patina, apply it at this time. Patinate the woven blank, the stamped blank, rivet disks, and 30cm of 26-gauge wire.

10 / Prepare the cuff for riveting

Mark the middle of the leather cuff on the top and bottom centered between the snaps. Put the stamped blank on top of the woven blank, making sure the rivet holes are aligned (photo p). Wrap tape around the top stamped blank and the bottom woven blank. Align the middle points of the blank with the middle of the cuff, and tape the blanks to the cuff. Using an awl, pierce the rivet holes through the leather, using the holes in the blank as a guide (photo q).

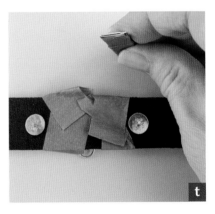

Remove the metal blanks and use the #54 drill bit to drill holes through the leather at the two pierced marks (photo r). Remove the tape, and align the rivet holes in the blanks with the leather holes. Tape the metal blanks to the cuff all the way around, making sure not to cover the rivet holes at the back.

11 / Prepare for riveting

I recommend practicing this technique with scrap metal before you go forward. Insert 1.5cm of flush-cut 16-gauge wire into each of the rivet holes (photo s). Place the two disks, stamped-side out,

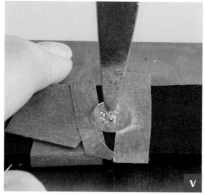

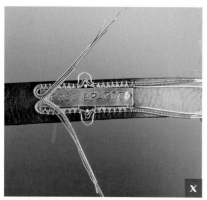

on the rivets on the back of the cuff, and grab the measuring tool made in step 4 (**photo t**). Tape the disks down, leaving the rivet wire free and clear. Place the measuring tool flush against the front of the cuff and the rivet wire, and adjust the rivet wire so it protrudes only as high as the tool. Flip the cuff over (don't change the position of the rivet wire at the front), and put the tool flush against the disk and against the wire. Flush-cut the wire so it is only as high at the tool (**photo u**).

12 / Rivet

Use the chiseled face of a riveting hammer to gently strike the opposide end of the wire on the back. Make sure the bench block is fully supporting the opposite end of the wire. The ends of the wire will begin to flare (**photo v**). Flip the cuff over, and hammer the rivet wire on the front the same way. Continue to flip and hammer perpendicularly to the last hammering action until the wire ends have sufficiently flared and is holding the assembly together

(**photo w**). Hammer both ends of the rivet with the flat face of the hammer to smooth out the rivets. Sand the rivets.

13 Frame with the weave

Arch the 20-gauge woven wires on the left end inward and then outward (**photo x**). Create a framing wave by forming the weave inward and outward in a large arch; keep the wires parallel (**photo y**). Coil the 20-gauge wire trios to the side of the center loop, making sure all the coils are side-by-side and not overlapping (**photo z**). Cut 15cm of 26-gauge wire. String a 2mm stone bead to the middle of the wire. Coil the wire on the upper and lower arched weave on the sides, keeping the bead centered on each end of the weave. Use your fingers to carefully form the completed assembly into a gentle curve. Support the metal blanks, and work slowly (**photo aa**). Try the cuff on and make sure the arch of the metal blanks conforms to your wrist (**photo bb**).

WOVEN NECK CUFF

A neck cuff is a substantial alternative to wearing a chain with handmade pendants. This versatile piece can be worn on its own or paired with a special pendant.

SUPPLIES

- 42cm 10-gauge dead-soft round copper wire
- 40cm 16-gauge dead-soft round copper wire
- 40cm 16-gauge dead-soft round silver wire
- 140cm 24-gauge dead-soft round silver wire

TOOLS

- Cast iron necklace mandrel
- Planishing hammer
- Bench block
- Metal file
- Sanding sponges in various grits
- Flexible tape measure
- Temporary blue painters tape
- Permanent marker
- Heavy-duty flush cutters
- Heavy-duty roundnose pliers
- Heavy-duty flatnose pliers
- Bracelet mandrel or soup can

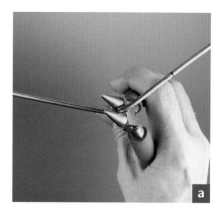
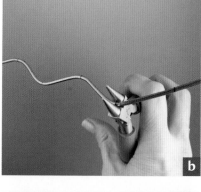
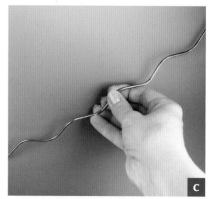
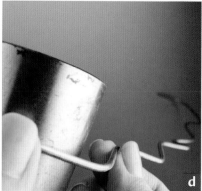
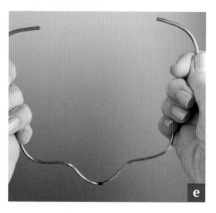
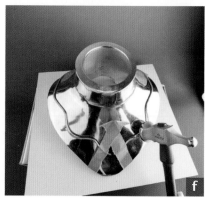

1 / Make the main frame

Cut 42cm of 10-gauge dead-soft round wire. Make a series of marks on the 10-gauge wire in the following order and from left to right: 7cm, 3.5cm, 3.5cm, 3.5cm, 3.5cm, and 3.5cm. Leave 7cm length on the right end. Using heavy-duty roundnose pliers, make an inward (valley) bend at the first mark on the left **(photo a)**. Make an outward (mountain) bend at the second mark on the left. Make a valley bend on the third mark. Make a mountain bend at the forth mark. Make a valley bend at the fifth mark **(photo b)**. Continue alternating valley/mountains bends at all the marks on the wire **(photo c)**. Turn the left and right 7cm ends inward using a bracelet mandrel or a soup can **(photo d)**. Hand-shape the cuff in a "U" shape, being careful to keep the bottom valley centered **(photo e)**. Place the main frame on the necklace mandrel, tape it down with blue painters tape, and hammer with a chasing hammer to slightly flatten and work-harden the wire **(photo f)**. Turn the ends of the main frame downward **(photo g)**, and hammer the ends into paddle shapes on a bench block **(photo h)**. File the ends

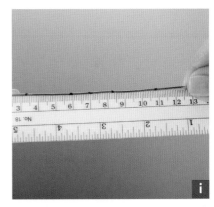

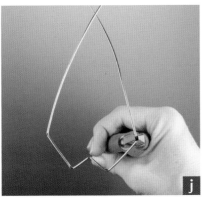

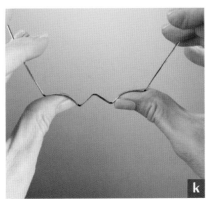

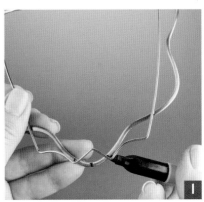

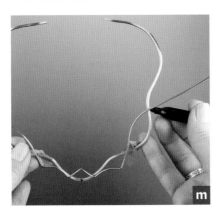

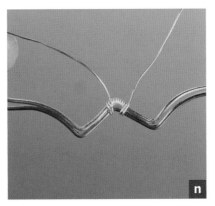

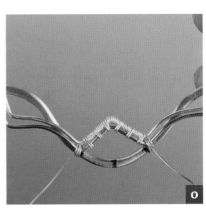

round, and sand the ends and the entire neck cuff.

2 / Prepare for the weave

Cut 40cm of 16-gauge dead-soft round copper wire, and mark the midpoint. Mark 12mm from the middle mark on the left and right side. Mark 2.5cm from the second mark on the left and right (**photo i**). With heavy-duty flatnose pliers, bend a mountain at the middle mark. Bend a valley at the 12mm marks, and bend the 2.5cm marks inward a little bit (**photo j**). Using your thumbs, arch the wire up between the second

and third marks (**photo k**). Align the 16-gauge wire where you want it to be woven to the main frame. For each time they cross over, make a mark on the main frame. This will help you remember to weave the wires together at that juncture (**photo l**). Once all the marks have been made, tape the two wires together at the areas where they cross to prepare for making the last wave. Press up with a thumb on the 16-gauge wire just after the last crossover. Mark on the main frame where the wires cross (**photo m**).

3 / Begin the weave

Cut 40cm of 16-gauge dead-soft round silver wire, and mark the midpoint. Mountain-fold the silver at the mark. Tape the silver mountain fold to the top of the copper mountain fold. Form the silver wire alongside the copper wire, mimicking its shape. Cut 140cm of 24-gauge weaving wire and, starting in the middle of the silver wire, coil around the top of the silver mountain fold seven times. Wrap the silver and copper wires twice on the left and right sides (**photo n**). Coil the silver wire five times on the left and right side. Wrap around the

73

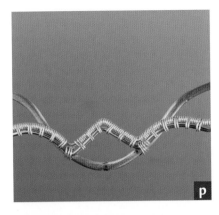
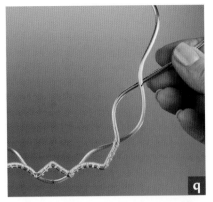
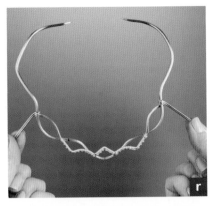

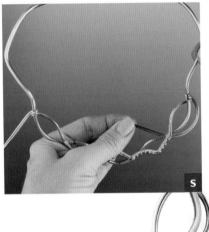

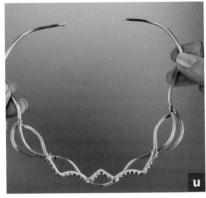

design variation

Secure a pendant to the center of the neck cuff with a heavy-gauge split jump ring, so the pendant can be replaced with another pendant for versatility.

copper and silver wires twice. Continue this coil-five/wrap-twice pattern until the weaving wire reaches a crossover mark. When that happens, wrap the copper wires together firmly three times (**photo o**). Continue the weave up to the next crossover marks on the left and right side (**photo p**).

4 / Make the arches

Arch the silver and copper wires across the entire upper main frame wave, and move under the main frame of the final crossover mark (**photo q**). Keeping the wires parallel, coil over, and then under the main frame (**photo r**). Bring the wires toward the outside of the main frame, form an arch, and cross under where the first arch originated (**photo s**). Pull both wires over and under the main frame and woven wires in a full coil (**photo t**). Cut the wire ends (**photo u**). Add patina, if desired.

LOOPY RING

This ring may look complex, but it is rather simple to make. Being familiar with "Continuous Loops," p. 19, will be very helpful. The ring resembles a zinnia flower, and any kind of round stone or metal bead can be included in the middle— as long as it fits inside the loops.

SUPPLIES

o 70cm 20-gauge dead-soft round wire
o 160cm 28-gauge dead-soft round wire
o 50cm 22-gauge dead-soft round wire
o 1 5–6mm round stone, pearl, or metal bead

TOOLS

o Wire Toolkit
o Ring mandrel
o 3mm and 4mm bail-forming pliers

design variation

Replace the bead with a pearl, use copper wire instead of silver, and patinate the metal to give a rich depth to the final appearance.

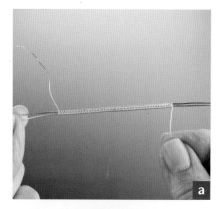

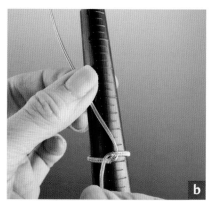

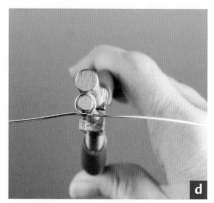

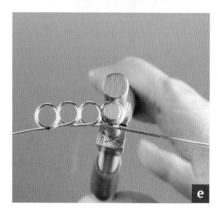

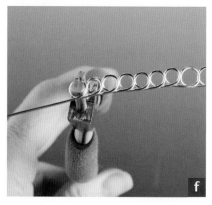

1 / Weave the ring shank

Weave the ring shank according to the size desired: 60mm for a size 8½ ring, 58mm for a size 7½ ring, 56mm for a size 6½ ring, and 53mm for a size 5½ ring. Cut two 35cm pieces of 20-gauge wire. Cut 100cm of 28-gauge weaving wire. Mark all three wires in the middle. Starting at the center of the two 20-gauge wires, weave a 2-1 weave with the middle of the 28-gauge wire (see "2-1 Weave," p. 20). Continue to the desired length **(photo a)**. Wrap the woven wires around a ring mandrel at the desired size, and hook the wires

together **(photo b)**. Swirl the wires together, keeping them close to the base of the ring shank **(photo c)**.

2 / Make two continuous loops

Cut 25cm of 22-gauge wire. Leaving a 3.5cm tail, create a 4mm loop with 4mm bail-forming pliers **(photo d)**. Make three more continuous loops with the 4mm bail-forming pliers **(photo e)**. Using 3mm bail-forming pliers, make seven more continuous loops next to the four larger loops **(photo f)**. Leave the 3.5cm tail intact. Make a second row of continuous loops with a second wire **(photo g)**.

3 / Connect the continuous loops with the ring shank

Coil the 3.5cm tail twice on the 3mm loop side of one continuous loop segment onto the double 20-gauge wires on the ring shank next to the swirl. Make sure loops are facing up **(photo h)**. Cut 25cm of 28-gauge weaving wire, and coil twice onto the 20-gauge wires to the left of the continuous loops near the swirl. Bring the wire through and around the first continuous loop, and then between the first two loops **(photo i)**. Continue to wrap the 28-gauge wire through and between each continuous loop

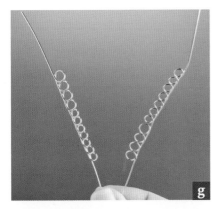

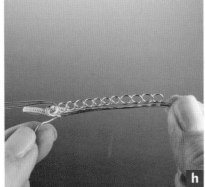

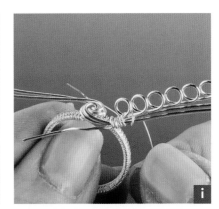

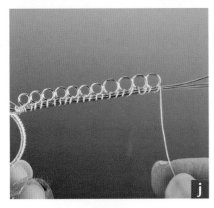

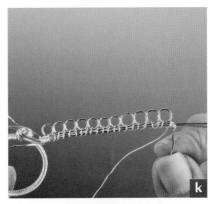

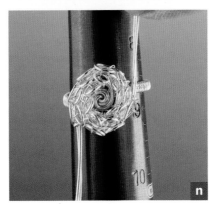

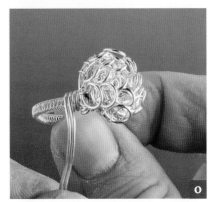

(photo j). Coil the 3.5cm end at the large loops onto the double 20-gauge wires (photo k). Trim the excess 28-gauge and 22-gauge wire ends. Repeat on the other side of the ring shank wires with the second continuous loop segment (photo l). Notice how all the loops are pointing upward.

4 / Swirl the continuous loops

Put the ring back on the ring mandrel, and swirl the loops just as was done with the ring shank wires earlier (photo m). Continue to swirl until all the continuous loops are swirled and one loop

wire end is pointing up and perpendicular to the ring shank and the other is pointing down (photo n). Wrap the wire ends around the ring shank twice, making sure to keep the wires parallel (photo o). Cut the 20-gauge wire ends.

5 / Add the bead

Cut 10cm of 28-gauge wire, and string a 4mm bead to the middle of the wire. Insert the bead in the middle of the continuous loop swirl. Thread the wire ends through the continuous loop and down to the ring shank (photo p). Coil the wire ends around the ring shank two times.

MOTHER'S EMBRACE NECKLACE

A friend was to become a grandmother, and she wanted a gift to give her daughter— something that would embody the warmth of being a new mother. After many prototypes, this elegant representation of mother and child holding each other became the final choice for that gift. Now, I share with you "Mother's Embrace," to be worn with love and affection.

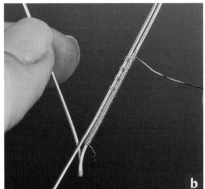

SUPPLIES

o 56cm 20-gauge dead-soft round
  silver wire

o 130cm 28-gauge dead-soft round
  silver wire

o 20cm 22-gauge dead-soft round
  silver wire

o 18 in. 1.5mm-link rolo chain, sterling
  silver, cut in half

o 7mm spring-loaded sterling silver clasp

o 6mm soldered sterling silver jump ring

o **2** 3mm sterling silver beads

o **1** 4mm sterling silver bead

o **1** 3mm round genuine pearl

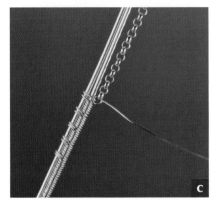

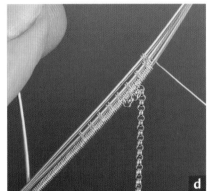

TOOLS

o Wire Toolkit

o File or sanding stick

o Straight pin

o Micro-needle chainnose pliers

o Tape measure

o Permanent marker

o Liver of sulfur (optional)

1 / Make the main frame

Cut 22cm of 20-gauge wire, and mark 10cm from one end. Bend the wire into a hard fold at the mark (see "Hard Fold," p. 12). Work-harden 1cm from the fold by grasping the parallel wires several times with flatnose pliers (don't mar the metal). Use your fingernails to open up the folded "V" front to back (not side-to-side). Don't open the 5mm nearest the fold.

NOTE: The right side of the "V" is 10cm long and the left side is 12cm.

2 / Coil the right side

Outer right frame wire: Cut 80cm of 28-gauge weaving wire, and starting at the end of the 28-gauge wire, coil 40 times onto the 10cm outer right frame wire. Start 5mm from the "V" **(photo a)**.
Middle right frame wire: Cut 10cm of 20-gauge wire, and finger-straighten the wire. Place this wire inside and parallel to the coiled wire. Allow about 7.5mm to extend below the "V". Double-wrap the weaving wire around the two 20-gauge

wires. Coil five times on the outer right frame. Create two more pairs of the two-wraps/five-coils pattern **(photo b)**. Wrap once around both wires, and on the second wrap, catch the end of a 9-in. piece of rolo chain and include it in the wrap **(photo c)**. Coil four coils, and catch the third link in the rolo chain. Coil the link to the right outer frame wire. (You are catching every other rolo chain link.) Wrap twice around both wires, and coil twice to the outer frame, catch the fifth link in the rolo chain, and coil it to the right outer frame twice. Repeat the wrap-two/coil-five pattern

two more times. Bring the weaving wire between the two frame wires.
Inner right frame wire: Cut 12cm of 20-gauge wire. Add this wire next to the inside 10cm wire, with a 7.5mm overhang below the bottom "V". Double-wrap the middle and the inner right frame **(photo d)**. Alternate double-wrapping the outer and middle wires with the middle and inner right frame wires for a total of 19 double wraps **(photo e)**. Carefully arch all the wires with your fingers into the "mother" side of the pendant (don't use a tool). Keep these wires parallel. Coil

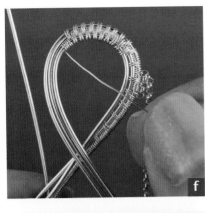

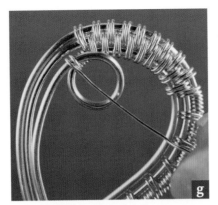

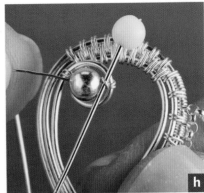

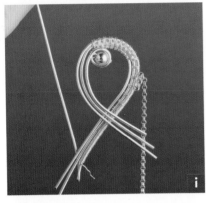

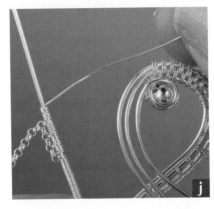

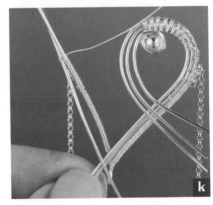

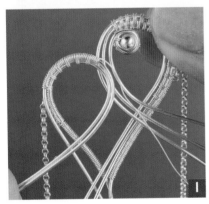

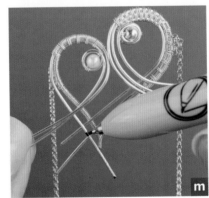

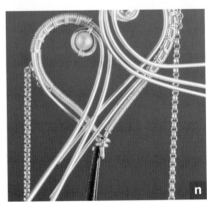

five times onto the inner frame wire at the end of the weave **(photo f)**.

"Mother" bead loop: Shift the inner wire counter-clockwise to create a loop large enough to fit a 4mm bead and a few wire wraps; use your fingers and tension (or 5mm bail-forming pliers) to form the loop. Wrap the loop twice with the weaving wire where it overlaps **(photo g)**. String a 4mm silver bead on the weaving wire, and nestle it within the loop. Coil twice on the other side of the loop, and then re-thread the wire through the bead and to the opposite side of the loop. This can be a little

difficult, as the wire tends to kink when bent into such a tight space; use a straight pin to keep the wire from kinking **(photo h)**. Coil the wire twice onto the inner right frame wire, and cut the weaving wire. Wrap the inner frame wire around the bead once to frame the bead. Form all the frame wires in a slightly tighter arch, so that they are all parallel and arch toward the bottom of the double-wrapped section of the middle and outer weave **(photo i)**.

3 / Coil the left side

Inner left frame wire: Cut 50cm of 28-gauge weaving wire, and coil 40 times onto the left frame wire. Start 5mm from the bottom "V". Catch the first link of a 9cm length of rolo chain, and coil it onto the left frame wire. Continue to coil every other link in the chain to the left side of the frame wire for a total of four links. Coil five more times without the chain **(photo j)**.

Outer left frame wire: Cut 12cm of 20-gauge wire, and finger-straighten it. Place that wire to the outside of the

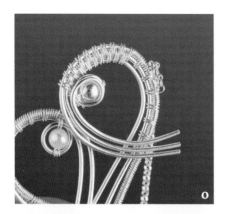

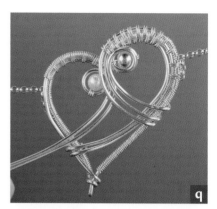

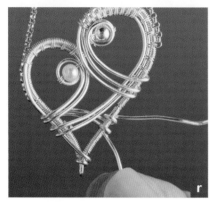

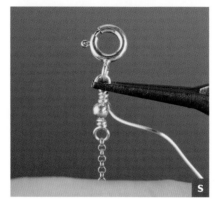

inner left frame wire. Allow 1.5cm of the wire to extend below the bottom "V". Wrap the inner and outer left frame wires together twice **(photo k)**. Create a total of six pairs of the wrap-two/coil-five pattern. Gently arch the two wires inward to create the "child" side of the pendant **(photo l)**.

"Child" bead loop: Create a loop by hand with the inner wire that is just large enough to fit a 3mm pearl and a few wire coils. Wrap the loop twice with the weaving wire where it overlaps, and string a 3mm pearl on the wire. Coil three times on the opposite side of the loop, and cut the weaving wire. Bring the inner wire around the pearl bead, or leave it unframed.

4 / Secure the wire ends

Left side: Mark the outer left frame wire at the bottom where the coil begins **(photo m)**. Using chainnose pliers, open and close the outer left wire to work-harden it (be careful not to mar the wire). Do not harden the wire below the mark. Coil the outer left frame wire twice around the lower "V" toward the peak **(photo n)**.

Right side: Cut all the "mother" frame wires even about 5mm from the edge of the outer weave **(photo o)**. Loop the three wires to the back using micro-needle chainnose pliers, and curl them into the weave **(photo p)**. Bring the lower middle and inner wires to the left side of the heart in a sweeping gentle arch, and use micro-needle chainnose pliers to secure the wire ends to the left frame wires **(photo q)**. Don't tighten too hard, or the left frame wires will indent (this is the reason why that wire was work-hardened).

Left side: Bring the left frame wires in front of and then behind the left side of the heart to create the "child's" head.

Then, arch the wires slightly downward with the pad of your thumb, so they reach the coiled outer frame on the right. Wrap both of those wires around the coiled outer frame once **(photo r)**. Be careful not to pull too tightly, causing an indent in the coil on the right side. Cut the excess 20-gauge wires.

5 / Secure the clasp to the chain

Add a clasp to the right side of the chain end with a 3mm bead between two secured basic loops (see "Secured Basic Loop," p. 13) **(photo s)**. Add a soldered ring to the left side of the chain with secured loops and a 3mm bead **(photo t)**. Tighten all coils and adjust any parts of the necklace that need attention. Patinate as desired.

VICTORIAN BLOSSOM BRACELET

The weaving technique used in this project is quick to accomplish and addictive.
Each component in this bracelet is completed with a similar weave with slight
variations. Mastering the continuous loop (see p. 19) will help you easily
create the focal point of this lovely bracelet.

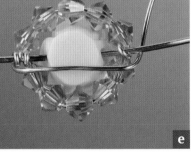

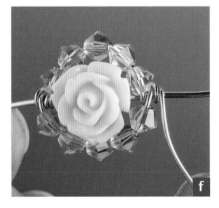

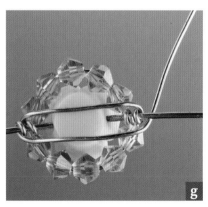

SUPPLIES

- o 61cm 20-gauge round dead-soft wire
- o 225cm 22-gauge round dead-soft wire
- o 120cm 28-gauge round dead-soft wire
- o **3** 10mm single-sided rose-shaped beads
- o **2** 6mm large-hole round pearls or beads
- o **24–26** 6º round seed beads
- o **22–26** 11º round seed beads
- o **40** 3mm crystal bicones
- o **30** 4mm crystal bicones
- o **3** 4mm contrasting crystal bicones
- o 15mm spring-loaded clasp

TOOLS

- o Wire Toolkit
- o 2mm bail-forming pliers
- o 5mm bail-forming pliers or roundnose pliers

NOTE: This bracelet measures about 8 in. long. Add or subtract links or make the loops larger or smaller as needed.

1 / Make flower links (make two)

Frame wire: Cut 11.5cm of 20-gauge wire, and mark in the middle.

Weave wire: Cut 40cm of 22-gauge weaving wire. Coil the end of this wire twice onto the 20-gauge frame wire to the left of the middle mark.

Weave with beads: String a rose-shaped flower bead, flower side up, onto the frame wire and against the coil. String five 4mm bicone crystals on the weav-ing wire. Arch the crystals around the rose bead, bringing the weaving wire on top of the other side of the frame wire **(photo a)**. Coil the weaving wire from the top, under, and over the top again **(photo b)**. It is essential to coil this way for every weave on each link. Cut the tail of the weaving wire. String another row of five 4mm bicones onto the weaving wire **(photo c)**, arch them around the other side of the rose on top of the frame wire, and coil once, top to bottom, and back on top again **(photo d)**.

Weave without beads: Bring the weaving wire underneath the rose and to the front of the frame wire on the other side **(photo e)**. Coil to the frame wire, top to bottom to top again, as with the last two coils **(photo f)**. Again, bring the wire to the back of the rose and to the top of the frame wire **(photo g)**. Coil the weaving wire to the frame wire on the top, under and top again **(photo h)**. Continue the weave for a total of four complete un-beaded weaves and one beaded weave (the beaded weave is around the flower) **(photo i)**. The weaves at the back are stacked side by side **(photo j)**.

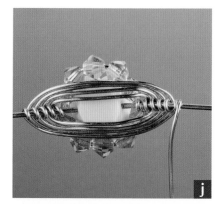

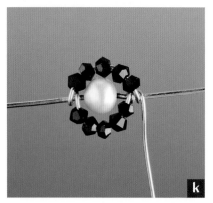

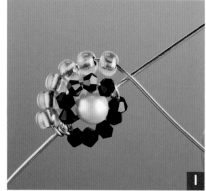

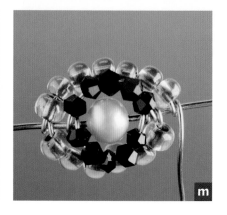

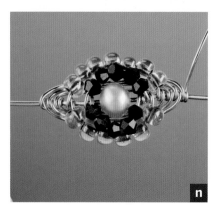

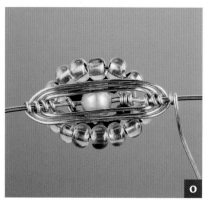

2 / Make pearl links (make two)

Make sure the hole in your pearl is big enough to accept 20-gauge wire (see "Drilling a Pearl Hole," p. 18), or use a different large-hole bead. Cut 11.5cm of 20-gauge wire, and mark in the middle. Slide the bead to the center of the frame wire. Cut 40cm of 22-gauge wire, and coil two time onto the 20-gauge frame wire to the left of the mark. String five 3mm crystal bicones on the 22-gauge weaving wire. Coil onto the opposite side of the pearl from the top. Always begin the coils from the top. Cut the short tail of the 22-gauge wire. Add

another row of bicones, and coil to the opposite side **(photo k)**. Add six or seven 6⁹ seed beads onto the weaving wire, and bring it above the bicones to the opposite side on top of the link **(photo l)**. Coil that weaving wire around the frame wire once. Add another row of seed beads to the bottom of the link, and coil onto the opposite side **(photo m)**. Wrap three more times on both sides for a total of two beaded weave sets and three un-beaded weave sets **(photo n)**. The back of the weave has all the wires side by side **(photo o)**.

3 / Make a flower focal link

Cut 15cm of 20-gauge wire, and mark the middle. Cut 50cm of 22-gauge weaving wire, and coil twice onto the 20-gauge frame wire to the left of the middle mark. String a flower bead to the middle of the frame wire. String five 4mm bicones, and coil once on the frame wire from the top. String another row of 4mm bicones, arch the wire to the other side, and coil from the top. String 10 3mm bicones, arch to the opposite side of the link, and coil once onto the frame wire. Add another row of 3mm bicones and coil from the top on the opposite side. Using 2mm bail-forming pliers, make a row of continuous loops on the weaving wire; start looping close to the coil on the frame wire. Make continuous loops to the opposite side, and coil once around the frame wire. Repeat the row of continuous loops for the opposite side **(photo p)**, coil once, and cut the weaving wire. There are no un-beaded weaves in the focal link. Cut 50cm of 28-gauge weaving wire, and coil to the 20-gauge

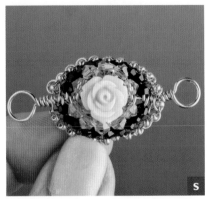

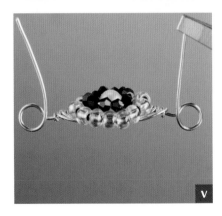

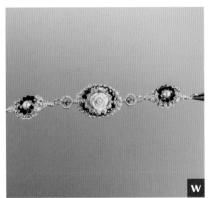

frame wire. Add an 11° seed beed to the weaving wire, and rest the bead on top of a continuous loop. Bring the weaving wire on top of the next loop, and coil once around the next loop and the first loop. Bring the wire back on top. Add another bead and nest it in the next loop **(photo q)**. Coil the weaving wire once around the edge of the current loop and the next loop. Bring the weaving wire to the top **(photo r)**. Continue to add a bead on top of each loop. When a full rotation has been achieved, coil twice to the frame wire. Cut the tail of the weaving wire. Create a secured loop parallel to the link on both ends of the focal

link using 5mm bail-forming pliers (see "Secured Basic Loop," p. 13) **(photos s and t, front and back of piece)**. Coil the secured loop on each end with 25cm of 28-gauge weaving wire. Cut 10mm of 28-gauge weaving wire, and coil onto the loop near the focal link, add a 4mm bicone, and coil on to the opposite side of the loop **(photo u)**. Trim the wire.

4 / Connect the links

Using 5mm bail-forming pliers, make a perpendicular loop to the ends of the pearl link **(photo v)**. Attach the loop to one side of the flower focal. Secure the loop. Secure the loop on the opposite

end of the pearl link **(photo w)**. Repeat for the flower link; make sure the loops are parallel. Repeat for the other side.

5 / Add the clasp

Cut 15cm of 22-gauge wire, and make a 5mm perpendicular loop about 4cm from one end. Insert that loop onto the end of one flower link, and secure with three or two coils. Add a 4mm bicone, and make another 3mm loop on the opposite side of the bead. Place the clasp onto the loop, and secure the loop with two or three coils **(photo x)**. Cut all wire tails.

INDEPENDENCE ROSE VESSEL

The great thing about vessels is that they can hold so many small and meaningful items. When I asked people what they would put into their vessel if they had one, and I heard, "tears," "hair," "beach sand," "blood," "pet ashes," "a message," "mustard seed," "a feather," "dandelion seed," and "glitter." What will you put in your vessel? Mine has small dried rosebuds, which I've sprayed with a little hairspray to prevent them from flaking.

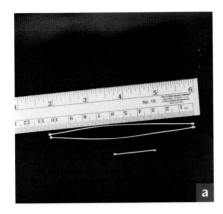

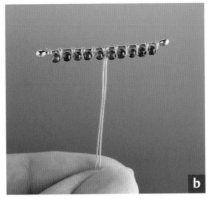

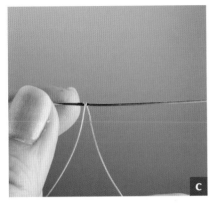

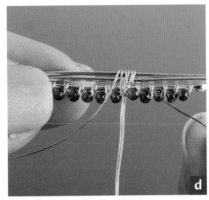

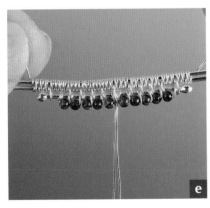

SUPPLIES

o 28cm 20-gauge dead-soft round wire

o 25cm 22-gauge dead-soft round wire

o 158cm 28-gauge dead-soft round wire

o **10–11** 2mm round stone beads

o Glass bottle with cork, any length, with a rim about 4cm circumference

o Vintaj patina in amethyst

o Small dried rosebuds sprayed with hairspray

TOOLS

o Wire Toolkit

o Torch Toolkit

o Paintbrush

o 11mm mandrel or dowel

o Sandpaper

also weave the bail.) Wrap this frame wire and the center of the beaded wire once with the weaving wire, and bring the weaving wire to the back. Add the second long frame wire, and wrap both long frame wires once. Coil the upper wire once. Coil the lower frame wire once. Wrap both the 20-gauge wires together (**photo d**) (see "2-1 Weave," p. 20). Continue the 2-1 weave, and each time the weaving wire reaches between two beads, wrap the bottom frame wire to the beaded wire between each bead, and then resume the 2-1 weave on the two long frame wires (**photo e**). Continue the 2-1 weave on the frame wires for three additional pairs of weaves to the left and right. The entire weave and beaded trim should measure 3cm. Since the next steps will be to wrap the weave around the bottle, patinate the wires now before attaching, if desired.

1 / Prepare the frame wires

Cut two 12cm pieces of 20-gauge wire, and torch-bead both ends (see "Torch-Beading a Wire End," p. 12). Mark the middle after beading the ends. Cut 4cm of 20-gauge wire, torch-bead both ends, and mark in the middle after beading the ends (**photo a**).

2 / Make the bead trim

Cut 18cm of 28-gauge weaving wire, and coil twice onto the left side of the torch-beaded 4cm wire. Wrap 9–11 2mm beads to the wire by adding a bead, coiling, and adding a bead until the wire and beads reach the end of the wire. Cut 15cm of 28-gauge weaving wire, coil twice at the center of the beaded wire, and leave the ends hanging straight down (**photo b**).

3 / Make the weave

Cut 125cm of 28-gauge weaving wire, and mark 30cm from one end. Starting at the mark on the weaving wire, coil in the middle of one of the long frame wires (**photo c**). (It is important to start the weave at the 30cm mark, as the other 95cm will be used not only to weave the rim of the vessel, but to

4 / Attach the weave to the rim of the bottle

Wrap the weave beneath and around the rim of the bottle with the beads facing downward (**photo f**). Bend the frame wires upward in the back where they meet (**photo g**).

design variation

Alternately, add a rounded bottle, add lengths of chain for fringe at the base of the weave, and increase the number of rows of the weave.

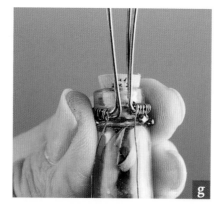

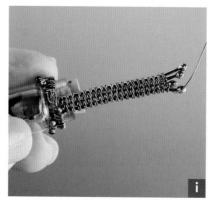

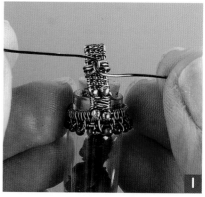

5 / Make the bail

String a 2mm bead on the longer weaving wire, and coil the weaving wire to the opposite side once **(photo h)**. Resume the 2-1 weave to 5mm from the end of all four frame wires **(photo i)**. Turn two of the torch-beaded wire ends inward. Weave a modified figure-8 for three weaves on the remaining two frame wires (see "Modified Figure-8 Weave," p. 20). Form the weave toward the back around an 11mm mandrel or dowel. Attach the 15cm weaving wire that was woven into the center around both torch-beaded ends two or three times **(photo j)**. That wire will hold the bail to the weave.

6 / Make the rose

Cut 25cm of 22-gauge wire, and wrap it around the middle front of the bail twice, bringing the wires forward **(photo k)**. Twist the wires together tightly **(photo l)**. Swirl the wires together two times **(photo m)**. Bring the wires together, and twist slightly. Coil once around the swirl. Every quarter turn, twist slightly and swirl the wire around the swirl until the rose is completed **(photo n)**. Separate the two wires to the left and right

(photo o). Coil the wires in opposite directions around the back of the bail **(photo p)**. Cut the wires and tuck them behind the rose.

7 / Paint the rose

Using Vintaj patina in amethyst, paint the rose with a soft paintbrush and allow it to dry **(photo q)**. Sand some of the colors off the top edges of the rose to give it more depth **(photo r)**. Add a chain, a charm with a jump ring, or a stamped message **(photo s)**.

design variation

If adding contents that can spill, such as liquids or fine powders, glue the cork to the inside of the bottle.

BE KIND
PENDANT

Antique shops, estate sales, garage sales, and resale stores all seem to have a plethora of silver-plated silverware. You may even get lucky and find a piece of silverware that is solid sterling silver. This pendant is just one of many jewelry ideas to make use of these eating utensils. In this lesson, we will cover cutting silverware, drilling silverware, and wire-weaving the handle.

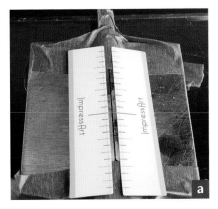

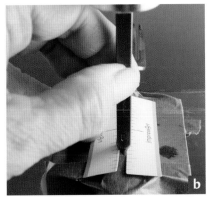

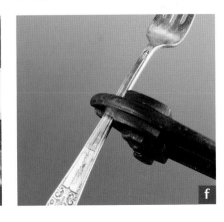

SUPPLIES

o Silver-plated spoon or fork with a flat handle and a blank surface

o 54cm 20-gauge silver dead-soft round wire

o 110cm 28-gauge silver dead-soft round wire

o 10cm 26-gauge wire

o **2** 7.5mm twisted soldered jump rings

o **2** 2mm round beads

o **1** 10mm briolette

o **1** 3mm pearl

TOOLS

o 11mm mandrel

o 3mm bail-forming pliers

o Progressively-finer grits of sandpaper

o Permanent marker

o Steel bench block

o Brass hammer

o Chasing hammer

o Metal alphabet stamps; 3mm lowercase italic and 3mm capitalized newsprint for rigid metals

o Drill or flexshaft and #61 drill bit

o Center punch

o Bolt cutters

o Protective glasses

o Metal file

o Temporary blue painters tape

o Impress Art Stamp Guide

o Ruler

1 / Secure the fork

Tape the fork down to a bench block with blue painters tape. Draw a line down the center of the handle with a ruler and permanent marker. Align two pieces of stamping-guide stickers on either side of the fork, leaving just enough space to stamp. Since the stamps are 3mm, leave 3mm between the guide stickers **(photo a)**.

2 / Stamp the fork

Since this stamping is done on a very strong metal, use a stamp set that is especially designed for rigid metals.

Unlike horizontal stamping, where the stamping begins in the middle, this stamping will begin at the bottom of the fork and goes upward. Place a "D" stamp at the bottom of the fork handle centered between the stamping guides, and give it one good strike with the brass hammer **(photo b)**. Stamp an "N" about 2mm above the "D" **(photo c)**. Repeat to stamp all four letters. Mark a horizontal line about 5mm up from the top of the "K" **(photo d)**. Put a stamping guide on the horizontal line, and stamp the word "be," with one letter on either side of the vertical line **(photo e)**.

Remove all the tape, and draw another horizontal line about 2cm up from the top of the word "be." Use bolt cutters to cut the handle at that line **(photo f)**. File and sand the edge of the cut handle.

3 / Drill weaving holes

Drilling requires a gentle hand—and protective eyewear. Also, drill bits are very thin, so please be cautious. Mark two evenly spaced holes 2mm down from the top of the handle, and mark two more 7mm below the top of the handle **(photo g)**. Using the brass hammer and center punch, make a divot at

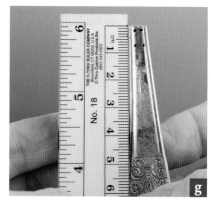
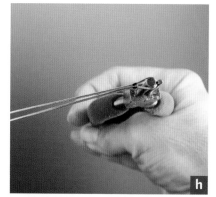
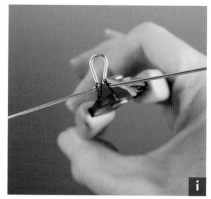
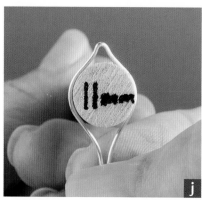
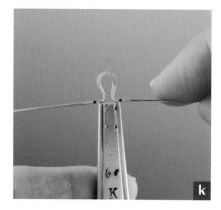
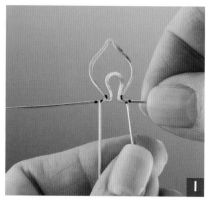
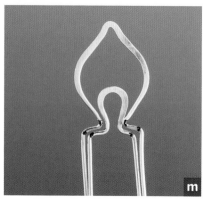
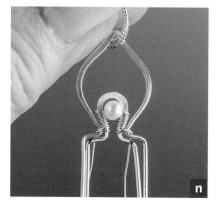

each mark. Drill holes at each divot with a #61 drill bit and drill press (see "Drilling Metal with a Drill Press," p. 16).

4 / Make the wire frame

Cut two 27cm lengths of 20-gauge wire, and mark the center of both. Make an open loop in the middle of one of the wires with 3mm bail-forming pliers **(photo h)**, and bend the wire ends outward 90 degrees at the base of the loop **(photo i)**. Soft-fold the second wire at its midpoint (see "Soft Fold," p. 12), and form it around an 11mm dowel to make an arabesque shape (see "Arabesque

Wire Shapes," p. 12) **(photo j)**. Using the chasing hammer and bench block, hammer the open loop and arabesque shape. Align the rounded wire on top of the handle and mark where the wire will bend down the side of the handle **(photo k)**. Bend the wires down at the marks. Put the arabesque shape on top of the rounded shape, and mark where that wire will drop down alongside the rounded wire **(photo l)**. Bend the arabesque shape wires downward, and make sure that both components fit together **(photo m)**. String the two jump rings onto the arabesque shape.

5 / Make the weave

Cut 110cm of 28-gauge weaving wire, string the pearl to the middle of the wire, and coil seven times to the left and right of the open-loop frame wire. Wrap around the base of the circle wire and the arabesque base twice **(photo n)**. Bring the wires through the top holes in the handle to the back **(photo o)**, and wrap the handle to both frame wires twice. Wrap around the frame wires twice **(photo p)**. Coil down the outer frame wire to the next holes in the handle, and double-wrap the frames to the second sets of holes. Double-wrap

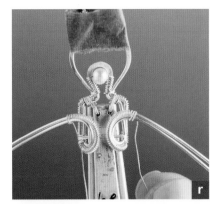

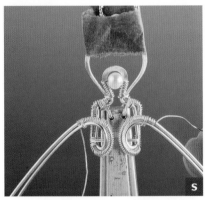

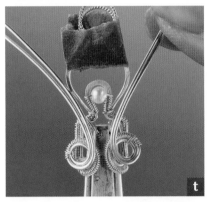

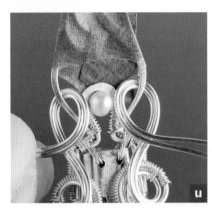

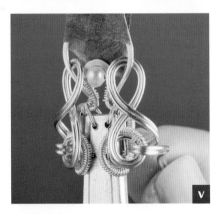

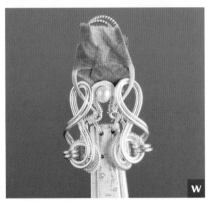

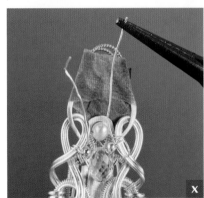

the two frame wires. Coil the outer frame wire down 1.5cm from the second hole (photo q). Wrap around both frame wires at the end of the coils.

6 / Make the loops

Arch both of the frame wires in and then outward with your fingers on the left and right side of the handle (photo r). Coil the outer frame wires three times, and cut the weaving wire (photo s). Loop the frame wire on the right clockwise and the left counter-clockwise in one full loop (photo t). Arch the frame wires backwards slightly. Loop them through the sides of the arabesque shape from the back, forming a loop (photo u). Bring the wire ends through the lower loop from the back, and wrap them one complete coil (photo v). Tighten the coils with micro-needle chainnose pliers (photo w).

7 / Attach the briolette

Cut 10cm of 26-gauge wire, and string a 2mm metal bead, a briolette, and another 2mm metal bead to the middle of the wire (photo x). Coil twice onto both sides on the upper loop, and secure the bead with two coils (photo y).

CICADA WING PENDANT

In early fall, I would walk with my son to grade school each morning. On the way, we would look for cicada shells and fallen cicadas. Now that he is grown, I still find myself seeking the cicadas. I have found a use for the bugs' wings, and while it may seem unusual, it is fascinating to think that one can imprint the wing onto metal. This lesson covers a lot of ground, including setting un-drilled gemstones, imprinting the wings, drilling metal, and wire-looping using your fingers. Disclaimer: No bugs were harmed in this project.

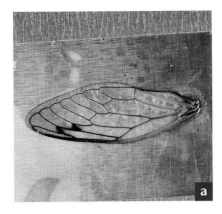

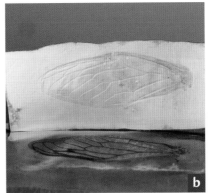

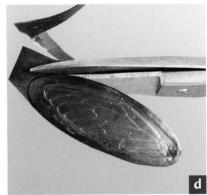

SUPPLIES

- o 75cm 20-gauge dead-soft round wire
- o 34cm 20-gauge half-hard round wire
- o 34cm 18-gauge dead-soft half-round wire
- o 70cm 24-gauge dead-soft round wire
- o 30cm 26-gauge dead-soft round wire
- o 185cm 28-gauge dead-soft round wire
- o 5x2cm 26-gauge dead-soft sheet metal
- o **2** cicada wings (one extra, in case the first imprint isn't perfect)
- o **5** 3mm faceted round gemstones
- o **2** 4mm open jump rings
- o **4** 4mm closed jump rings
- o **6** 2mm beads
- o **2** 3mm round beads
- o **1** 4mm faceted gemstone bead
- o **1** 7x5mm briolette

TOOLS

- o Wire Toolkit
- o Torch Toolkit
- o Scribe, etching, or engraving pen
- o Drill or flexshaft and drill bit #65
- o 1.5x3.8cm oval template
- o Metal shears
- o Center punch
- o Liver of sulfur
- o Permanent marker
- o Sanding sponge
- o Clear packing tape
- o Hammer and steel bench block
- o Steel wool #0000
- o Spring clamp with rubber tips
- o Temporary blue painters tape

1 / Emboss the cicada wing

Tape a piece of packing tape, sticky side up, onto a bench block with blue painters tape. Lay the cicada wing onto the sticky surface of the tape, and carefully burnish it with your fingers to get as many air pockets out as possible (**photo a**). Place the 5.5x2cm sheet metal on top of the wing, and burnish it onto the tape. Tape the metal onto the bench block, and hammer the metal vigorously in all areas where the wing is located. Using one side of the taped area as a hinge, lift up the metal to see if you are happy with the embossing (**photo b**). If not, allow the hinged tape to keep the metal in place, and hammer again. Use an oval template to make an oval around the perimeter of the wing, making sure to allow for room for drilled holes above and below the wing. Patina the metal with liver of sulfur so the lines are more visible.

2 / Engrave the wing

Use an engraving pen or scribe like a ballpoint pen, and follow all the lines in the wing. The pen's hard, very sharp stylus can cut into the metal to deepen the lines (**photo c**).

3 / Cut the metal

Using metal shears, cut the oval shape around the wing. Make sure that there is plenty of clearance for the drilled holes (**photo d**). File and sand the edges of the metal smooth, and use the #0000 steel wool to clean up the wing surface.

4 / Drill the holes

Mark three evenly spaced marks on top and the bottom edges of thte oval. Make sure one of the marks in the middle on both the top and bottom. Center-punch all the marks. Using a #65 drill bit and drill or flexshaft, drill a hole at each mark (**photo e**). Arch the metal wing with your fingers slightly to give it dimension.

5 / Set the gemstones

Cut two 17cm pieces of 20-gauge half-hard round wire. Cut two 17cm pieces of 18-gauge half-round wire. Mark 5cm from one end of all four wires. Tape

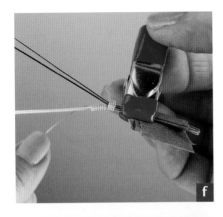 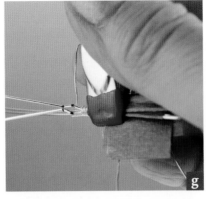 

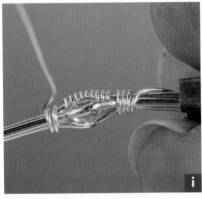 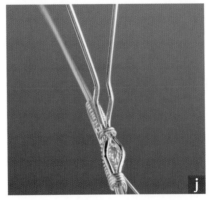 

 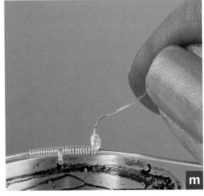 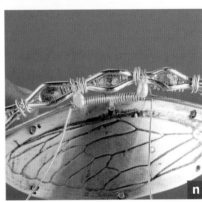

the four wires together with the two round wires on the bottom and the two half-round wires on top with the dome facing upward. Clamp the stacked wires with a spring clamp. Cut 70cm of 24-gauge weaving wire, and coil all four wires together at the 5cm mark. Bend the half-round 18-gauge wires up a bit, and coil the weaving wire around the two round wires nine times **(photo f)**. Mark the half-round wires 3mm and 6mm from the original coil, bend the 3mm marks inward, and bend the 6mm marks outward, forming a diamond shape. Open the wires slightly **(photo**

g). Turn the wires upside down and insert a 3mm gemstone with the culet, or pointed end facing down into the diamond-shaped wire **(photo h)**. Wrap the weaving wire tightly around all four wires twice, while supporting the stone position with your thumb and index finger, making sure the table (flat part of the gemstone) is flat against the coil **(photo i)**. Flip the weave upright again. Bend the half-round wires up, create another 3mm and 6mm diamond, and coil nine coils on the round wire with the weaving wire **(photo j)**. Insert a 3mm gemstone, and follow the above

directions to secure the stone. Create a total of five gemstone diamonds, and end with four coils on the round wire at the end of the sequence. Bend the round wires up at a 90-degree angle on the left and right sides of the gemstone section **(photo k)**. Cut the half-round wires close, and tuck the ends around the round wires in a coil. Using 3mm bail-forming pliers, make a bail loop toward the back with the round wires **(photo l)**. Wrap the round wire ends around the base of the bail twice, and cut the 20-gauge wire ends. Make this bail loop on both ends of the segment.

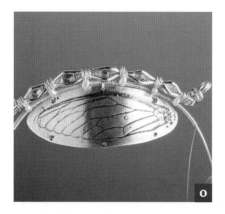

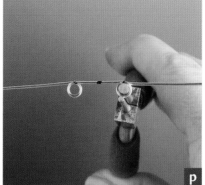

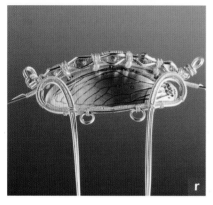

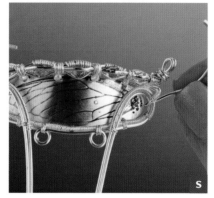

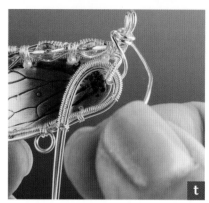

6 / Make the top weave

Cut 20cm of 20-gauge dead-soft round wire, and mark the middle. Cut 85cm of 28-gauge weaving wire and, beginning in the middle of the weaving wire, wrap twice around the 20-gauge frame wire and the center hole on the top of the wing. Coil 13 times onto the frame on the left and the right. String a 2mm bead or pearl onto the weaving wire on the left and the right sides **(photo m)**. Wrap the weaving wire twice between the gemstones on the right and left of the center, and bring the weaving wire to the back and then toward the front **(photo n)**. Continue coiling and wrapping to the last hole on each end, and wrap the hole and frame wire twice on the left and right sides. End the sequence with 20 coils on the frame wire on both sides **(photo o)**.

7 / Make the bottom weave

Cut 27cm of 20-gauge dead-soft wire for the inner bottom frame, and mark in the

middle. Cut 100cm of 28-gauge weaving wire, and wrap twice around the center lower wing hole and the middle of the inner bottom frame wire. Coil 27 times to the left and the right of the frame wire. Cut 28cm of 20-gauge dead-soft wire. Mark the middle and then 7mm to the left and right of the midpoint. Using 3mm bail-forming pliers, make a downward loop at both 7mm marks **(photo p)**. Wrap the weaving wire three times through the loops on the left and right side. Make 16 (you may need more or fewer coils) coils on the left and right side of the inner bottom frame wire. Make three wraps just before the left and right wing holes, then wrap the inner bottom frame wire and the wing hole twice. Coil 17 times on the inner frame, double-wrap both frame wires, and then coil 60 times on the outer loop frame wire on the left and right sides **(photo q)**.

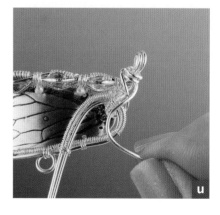

8 / Create loops

Arch the bottom frame wires inward in a teardrop-shaped loop, so that the arch reaches the gemstones. Using the weaving wire, secure the loop to the frame by wrapping around the loop and the frame **(photo r)**. Encircle the ends of the upper frame wires in front and to the back of the lower teardrop loops **(photo s)**. Bring that wire up and around the bail **(photo t)**, and create an "S" wave **(photo u)**. Insert the wire end

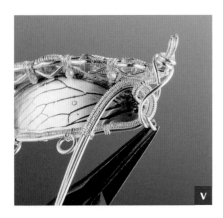

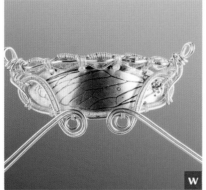

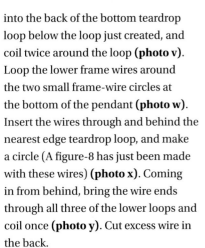

into the back of the bottom teardrop loop below the loop just created, and coil twice around the loop **(photo v)**. Loop the lower frame wires around the two small frame-wire circles at the bottom of the pendant **(photo w)**. Insert the wires through and behind the nearest edge teardrop loop, and make a circle (A figure-8 has just been made with these wires) **(photo x)**. Coming in from behind, bring the wire ends through all three of the lower loops and coil once **(photo y)**. Cut excess wire in the back.

9 / Wrap the briolette

Cut 15cm of 26-gauge wire. Create a briolette wrap (see "Briolette Wrap and Dangle," p. 14), and coil the briolette wire down upon the briolette several times. String a 4mm gemstone bead and make a 2mm loop at the top of the gemstone. Set this aside for now. Cut 15cm of 26-gauge wire, and string a 3mm

bead, the loop above the briolette, and another 3mm bead to the center of the wire. Coil both wire ends twice around the insides of the lower frame-wire loops, and coil twice next to the bead in a secured-bead coil **(photo z)**.

10 / Finish

Insert two soldered twisted jump rings onto an open jump ring, and place the open jump ring onto the bail loop. Repeat on the other side of the pendant.

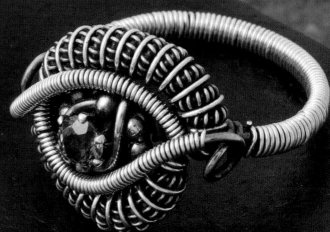

SWIRL GEMSTONE RING

You'll work with undrilled gemstones and incorporate them into a weave with this pretty little ring. This piece can easily become a pendant or bracelet, too; simply create a bail or secured loops in place of the ring shank.

SUPPLIES

- o **1** 4mm round gemstone
- o Snap-Set 4mm 6-prong silver setting
- o 50cm 20-gauge dead-soft round wire
- o 28cm 22-gauge dead-soft round wire
- o 60cm 26-gauge dead-soft round wire
- o 40cm 26-gauge dead-soft round wire in a contrasting color
- o 120cm 28-gauge dead-soft round wire
- o 50cm 28-gauge dead-soft round wire in a contrasting color
- o **10** 2mm sterling silver beads

TOOLS

- o Wire Toolkit
- o Ring mandrel
- o 20-gauge and 22-gauge steel wire mandrels
- o Hammer
- o Bench block

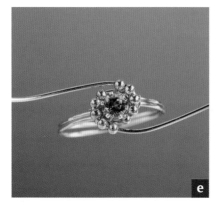

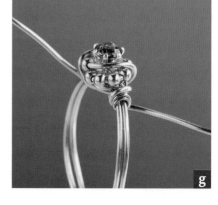

NOTE: Choose a ring size 1.5cm larger than the desired ring size. Coiling will decrease the size.

1 / Make the ring shank

Cut 50cm of 20-gauge wire, and wrap it twice around the ring mandrel at the desired size. Hook the wires together tightly on the mandrel (**photo a**). Swirl the wires together (**photo b**), and then lightly hammer it to flatten.

2 / Add the gemstone

Insert the culet (point) of a 4mm gemstone into the setting, and press down firmly with your finger. The gemstone will snap into place. Cut two 10cm pieces of 28-gauge wire, and place them parallel to each other through the setting (**photo c**). Balance the flat gemstone setting on the hammered swirl, and coil the 28-gauge wires onto the ring shank. Swirl the 20-gauge wires up around the setting (**photo d**).

3 / Add beads

String five 2mm beads on both sides of the 20-gauge wires, and swirl until the beads make a circle around the setting (**photo e**). Bring both wires across the

sides of the gemstone, and tuck them down between the first and second beads (**photo f**). Coil the 20-gauge wires onto the ring shank once (**photo g**).

4 / Coiled coil (make two)

Cut 50cm of 28-gauge wire, and coil onto the center of a 14cm piece of 22-gauge wire. Leave both ends of the 22-gauge wire uncoiled. Coil this coiled wire onto a 20-gauge wire mandrel or directly onto a 20-gauge wire on the ring shank. Continue until all the coiled 22-gauge wire has been coiled into a link (**photo h**). Cut 20cm of 26-gauge

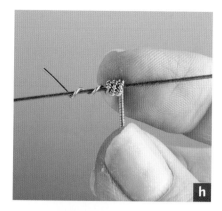

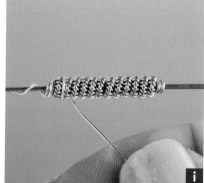

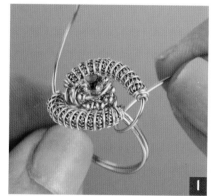

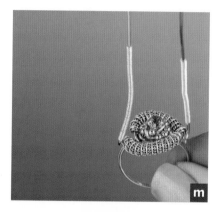

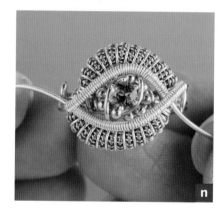

wire in a contrasting color. Coil it around the base of the coiled link, and then wrap it between the the coils of the coiled link **(photo i)**. Continue to coil the 26-gauge wire onto the opposite side of the link. Cut the ends of all the coiled bead wires. String the link onto the 20-gauge wire on one side of the ring shank, and slide it to the gemstone **(photo j)**. Swirl the coils around the gemstone until the ends meet **(photo k)**. Coil the ends of the wires onto the ring shank once, and bring wires straight up **(photo l)**.

5 / Add accent coils

Cut two 25cm pieces of 28-gauge wire in a contrasting color, and coil each onto one of the 20-gauge wires **(photo m)**. Bring each contrasting coil across the ring and into the groove between the coiled link and the gemstone, and tuck on either end **(photo n)**. Make a loop on the side of the ring, bring the ends down to the ring shank, coil twice, and cut the wire **(photo o)**.

6 / Coil the ring shank

Cut 60cm of 26-gauge wire. Coil onto the shank until it's fully covered **(photo p)**.

design variation

Add 3mm beads instead of 2mm beads for a more prominent beaded center.

FORGET-ME-NOT PENDANT

Forget-me-not flowers are petite, blue blossoms with the genus name of Myosotis, which in the Greek language means, "mouse ear." The five petals of the flower symbolize true love and connections that last a lifetime. This lesson is both a necklace and a main component for the following cuff (see p. 106). Consider making a practice flower from copper or other non-precious metal, as it takes a little time to master the technique.

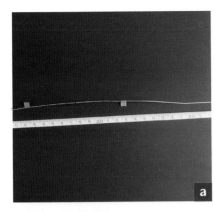

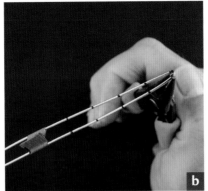

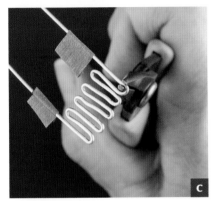

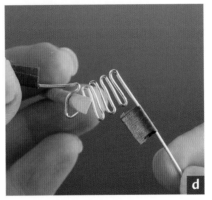

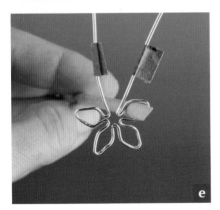

SUPPLIES

- o 65cm 20-gauge wire
- o 5cm 18-gauge wire
- o 95cm 28-gauge wire
- o 15cm 22-gauge wire
- o 15cm 28-gauge copper or scrap wire
- o 7cm bead (2mm) chain
- o **1** 15mm round low-dome cabochon
- o **1** 4mm round bead
- o **2** 3mm round beads
- o **1** 7x4mm briolette
- o Assorted centered-drilled beads and spacers that will fit on 22-gauge wire.

TOOLS

- o Wire Toolkit
- o Temporary blue painters tape
- o 3mm and 16mm dowels or mandrels
- o Chasing hammer
- o Steel bench block
- o 5mm bail-forming pliers

1 / Create the flower

Cut 35cm of 20-gauge wire. Mark the middle of the wire, and then mark five 1cm increments to the left of the midpoint mark and five 1cm increments to the right. You should have a total of 11 marks. Tape the last mark on the left and the right sides (the tape is a reminder not to fold) **(photo a)**.

NOTE: For this project, a valley-fold looks like a "V" and a mountain-fold looks like a mountain peak.

Beginning at the center mark of the 20-gauge wire, make a valley-fold **(photo b)**. Mountain-fold to the left and the right of the valley fold. Valley-fold on the marks next to the mountain folds. Continue the alternating mountain-/valley-folding until all the marks are folded except for the taped marks **(photo c)**. Be sure the straight wire ends are pointing downward at this point. Insert a 3mm dowel into the first valley-fold on the left, and form the fold around the dowel to create a petal (see "Arabesque Wire Shape," p. 12) **(photo d)**. Place the dowel into the next

valley-fold, and create a second petal. Continue to make four petals in each of the valley-folds **(photo e)**. Remove the blue tape. Now the flower needs to be stabilized: Take 15cm of scrap 28-gauge wire, and weave it around the center of the petals for a temporary hold **(photo f)**. Bring the straight wires around either side of the 3mm dowel, and twist them together at the marks **(photo g)**.

2 / Make the flower frame

Cut 30cm of 20-gauge wire, and mark the middle. Form the wire around a 16mm dowel, and twist the ends

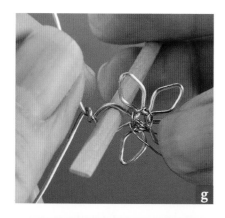
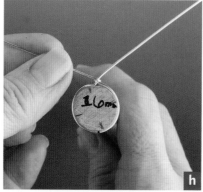
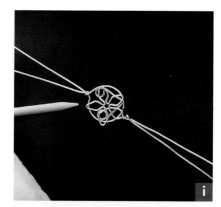

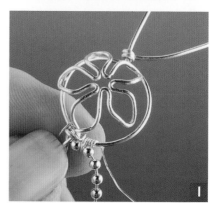

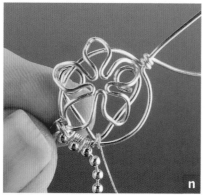
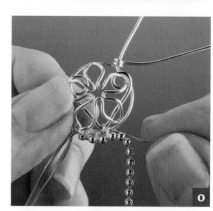

together opposite the middle mark **(photo h)**. Slightly hammer the circle only (not the twist) to work-harden it.

3 / Make the heart

Cut 5cm of 18-gauge wire, and soft-fold the wire in the middle (see "Soft Fold," p. 12). With 3mm bail-forming pliers, make an inward loop on either end. Hammer the heart slightly to work-harden it. This photo shows how the flower, the frame and the heart will layer during weaving. Note the heart is at the back of the pendant **(photo i)**.

4 / Fit the flower

Slightly arch each petal downward using an arching motion with the chainnose pliers at each flower tip. Be sure the arched petals fit around the cabochon **(photo j)**.

5 / Weave the flower

Place the flower on top of the frame with the straight wires of the flower opposite the straight wires of the frame. Cut 80cm of 28-gauge weaving wire, and coil the end of the wire twice around the flower-twist. Coil onto the frame twice. Cut 7cm of bead chain. Wrap

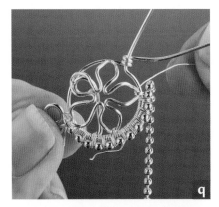

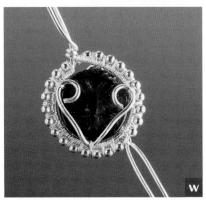

between the first two beads onto the frame twice **(photo k)**. Coil four times onto the frame **(photo l)**, and then wrap between the next two beads onto the frame twice **(photo m)**. Coil twice onto the frame, and then wrap the frame to the point of the heart twice **(photo n)**. Double-wrap the frame between the next two beads **(photo o)**. Continue to coil four to the frame, wrapping twice between the beads, until the weaving wire reaches the next petal. Wrap the petal to the frame twice **(photo p)**. Continue to coil four on the frame and wrap two between the beads until the wire reaches the next petal; wrap twice around the petal **(photo q)**. When the weaving wire reaches the loop of the heart, wrap the loop twice to the frame with the weaving wire **(photo r)**. Wrap twice between the beads in the chain **(photo s)**. Continue to coil four on the frame and wrap two between the beads. Stretch the bead chain across the frame twist—or, alternatively, cut the chain and resume the wrap on the opposite side of the twist. When the weaving

wire reaches the next petal, stop. Insert the 15mm cabochon and push it firmly inside. It is a tight fit, but it will work. Once the cabochon is inside, wrap the wire twice around the petal and the frame **(photo t)**. Continue weaving and wrapping, catching the last petal and the other loop of the heart **(photo u)**. Cut the weaving wire when you have reached the flower twist **(photos v and w, front and back)**.

NOTE: To complete the Forget-Me-Not Cuff, p. 106, stop here and leave the wire ends extended.

6 / Add a bottom dangle and top bead embellishment

Create a secure loop at the top and bottom of the pendant with 3mm bail-forming pliers (see "Secured Basic Loop," p. 13). Cut 15cm of 22-gauge wire, and add a dangle to the bottom loop with an assortment of beads and a 7x4mm briolette (see "Briolette Wrap and Dangle," p. 14). Add a bead swag to the top of the pendant between two petals with 15cm 28-gauge wire, and a 4mm and two 3mm beads. Coil the swag onto the frame twice **(photo x)**. Patinate, if desired.

FORGET-ME-NOT CUFF

This elaborately wired cuff is a great way to practice working with many wires at one time. At one point in the project, you will be working with 20 different wire ends. The photos and instructions will show you how to organize the process and break down the cuff into different components. Refer to the Forget-Me-Not Pendant, p. 102, to make the center focal component of the cuff.

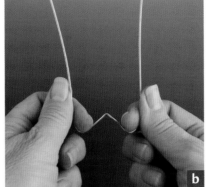

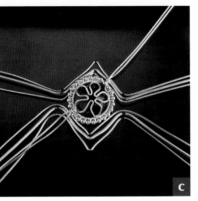

NOTE: Make mirrored left and right, and upper and lower sections.

1 / Make two soldered rings

Cut 14cm of 16-gauge wire, and coil it 2½ times onto a 16mm dowel. Flush-cut the coil to make two rings. Use a butane torch to solder both of the rings at the seam with easy solder and flux (see "Soldered Ring," p. 15).

2 / Make the frames

Cut two 30cm pieces of 16-gauge wire, and mark and soft-fold at the middle (see "Soft Fold," p. 12). Cut two 40cm pieces of 18-gauge wire, mark the middle, and bend at a 90-degree angle at the mark. Cut two 30cm pieces of 20-gauge wire, mark the middle, and bend at a 90-degree angle at the mark. Shape the 16-gauge center wire around a 2.5cm dowel; wrap only halfway around the dowel for each dead-soft round wire. Stack the wires together with the 18-gauge wire on top, the 16-gauge wire in the middle, and the 20-gauge wire on the inside; form the 18-gauge and

20-gauge wires alongside the 16-gauge form **(photo a)**. Mark 2cm on the left and right of the peak on both 16-gauge wires. Using your fingers, bend upward at those 2mm marks to make a sort of "U" wave **(photo b)**. Re-stack the wires with the 18-gauge wire on top, the 16-gauge wire in the middle, and the 20-gauge wire on the inside, and again, form these wires alongside the 16-gauge wire. Place the Forget-Me-Not component in the center of the frame wires, with the Forget-Me-Not wires at the 2 o'clock and 8 o'clock positions **(photo c)**. Make sure the wires allow room for

the component. Make sure the upper and lower frame wires "U" waves will allow room for a 4mm bead; adjust so the 4mm bead will fit between them. On the 16-gauge wire, create a half-circle shape with a 16mm dowel next to the "U" wave **(photo d)**. Place the soldered jump rings into the space made with the dowel, and make sure the top and bottom 16-gauge frame wires fit nicely around the jump ring **(photo e)**. Form the 18-gauge frame wire on outside of the 16-gauge frame wire. Form the 20-gauge frame wire on the inside of the 16-gauge frame wire. The weaving will pull these wires closer together, so don't worry if they are a little off. The main thing is to shape the 16-gauge wire well.

3 / Begin weaving the frame

Cut 300cm of 28-gauge weaving wire for the upper weaving wire, and cut 400cm of 28-gauge wire for the lower weaving wire. String a 3mm stone bead to the center of the upper weaving wire, and

SUPPLIES

- o Forget-Me-Not component, p. 102
- o 82cm 16-gauge dead-soft round wire
- o 90cm 18-gauge dead-soft round wire
- o 60cm 20-gauge dead-soft round wire
- o 840cm 28-gauge dead-soft round wire
- o **2** 3mm round metal beads
- o **2** 3mm faceted round stone beads
- o **2** 4mm faceted round stone beads
- o 4.5x2.5cm dead-soft sterling silver sheet metal

TOOLS

- o Wire Toolkit
- o Soldering Toolkit
- o Micro-needle chainnose pliers
- o Dapping block and daps
- o Disk cutter, or shears and 19mm circle template
- o 9mm, 16mm, and 25mm dowels or mandrels
- o Metal patterning tools (optional)
- o Brass hammer
- o 1.25mm metal hole punch or drill press and drill bit #60
- o 2mm and 3mm bail-forming pliers

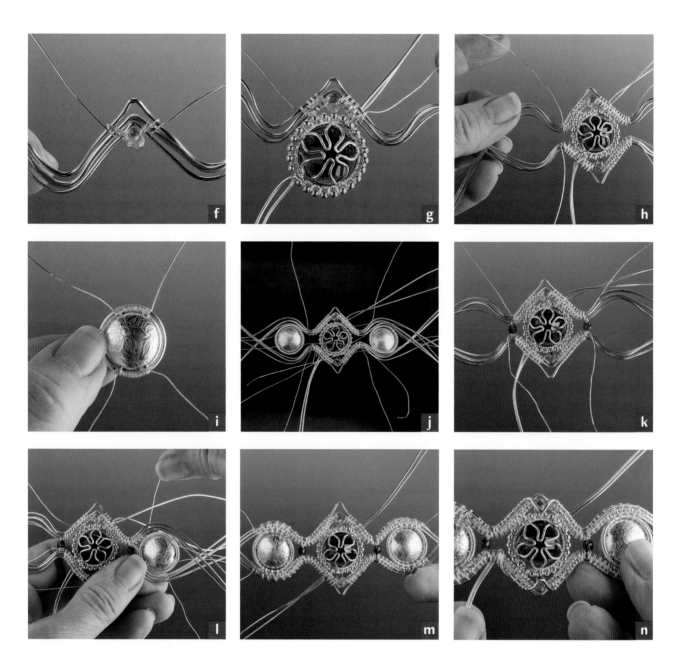

coil one time around either side of the peak of the 20-gauge frame wire. Add the 16-gauge frame wire, double-wrap the weaving wire around both wires, and bring the weaving wire between the frame wires. Add the 18-gauge frame wire, and double-wrap around the 16-gauge and the 18-gauge wires **(photo f)**. Bring the weaving wire behind the three wires. This is the frame weave sequence. Weave 2½ more sets of weaves, and double-wrap the component between two beads to the 20-gauge frame wire **(photo g)**. Double-wrap the 20-gauge inner frame wire to the

16-gauge wires. Double-wrap the middle 16-gauge wire to the outer 18-gauge frame wire. Double-wrap the 16-gauge frame wire to the 20-gauge frame wire. Double-wrap the 20-gauge frame wire to the component. Weave about seven more sets of double-wraps on the three frame wires to the bottom of the "U" wave **(photo h)**.

4 / Make the metal domes

Pattern the 4.5x2.5cm 26-gauge sheet as desired. Anneal the metal (see "Annealing," p. 12). Cut two metal disks from the patterned metal with a 19mm disk

cutter and a brass hammer (see "Disk Cutting," p. 16). (If you don't own a disk cutter, use a 19mm circle template and metal shears to cut out the two disks.) Using a 1.25mm metal hole punch (or a #60 drill bit and drill press), punch two holes into the disks at the top, 6mm apart and two holes in the bottom, 6mm apart. Place the drilled disks, pattern-side down, into a dapping block and dap the disk into a dome. Next, you'll need the two soldered rings from earlier and the two domes. Cut four 35cm pieces of 28-gauge weaving wire. For both rings: Mark the ring, and then make another

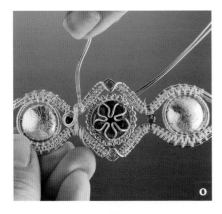

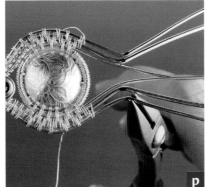

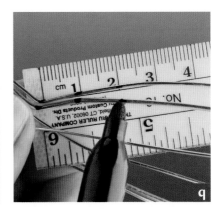

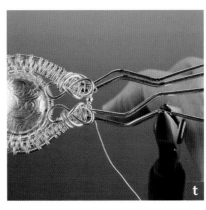

mark directly across from the first mark. Beginning in the middle of one 35cm piece of weaving wire, coil eight times to the left and right of one mark for a total of 16 coils. Repeat at the other mark. Double-wrap the weaving wires through the holes in the dome, and continue to coil for three more coils on each side (**photo i**). Do not cut the weaving wires. Place the coiled domes with coils facing left and right (not top and bottom), next to the focal component. Re-shape all the frame wires so they fit nicely around the coiled domes (**photo j**). Remember to leave room between the domes and focal component for a 4mm bead. Attach a 4mm bead on the left and right of the focal component at the center of the "U" wave with the weaving wire. Coil the bead to the opposite side of the "U" wave. Re-string the bead and return the wire to its original position (**photo k**).

5 / Continue weaving

Weave three more sets of two-wrap weave on the frame wires. When the weaving wire reaches the top of the

domed ring, start including it in the two-wrap weave (**photo l**). Follow this pattern: Double-wrap the ring and 20-gauge frame wire, bring the wire between the ring and the frame wire. Double-wrap the 20-gauge frame wire and 16-gauge frame wire, bring the wire between the 20-gauge and the 16-gauge frame wires. Double-wrap the 16-gauge frame wire and the 18-gauge frame wire, and bring the wire behind the weave and between the ring and the 20-gauge frame wire. Double-wrap the 20-gauge frame and the 16-gauge frame wires, and bring the weaving wire behind the weave and into the ring. Double-wrap the ring and the 20-gauge frame wire, and continue the sequence to the other side of the domed disk. With the remaining wire on the ring coils, finish coiling the exposed ring, and trim the weaving wires (**photo m**).

6 / Loop the frame wires

Bring the bottom pair of component frame wires behind the weave and toward the "U" wave, and coil once

just before the indent of the "U" wave (**photo n**). Pull the two wires up, make a complete loop around the 4mm bead, and then coil to the opposite side of the indent in the "U" wave (**photo o**). Bring the wires to the back, trim, and use micro-needle chainnose pliers to tuck the wires inward. Repeat on the other component frame wires in a mirror image.

7 / Make the side diamond

Mark for the diamond: Measure about 1cm from the edge of the dome and ring, make a mark on the 16-gauge and the 18-gauge (not the 20-gauge) frame wires, and turn those marked wires outward (**photo p**). Make another mark 1cm from the bend and a third mark 1cm from the second mark (**photo q**). Loop the 20-gauge frame wire outward and then in toward the dome. Cross the 20-gauge frame wire in a sort of figure-8. Bring the wire behind the weave, then in front of the weave, and insert the wire end into the figure-8 loop closest to the dome. Coil the wire to the weave and back through the figure-8 loop (**photo**

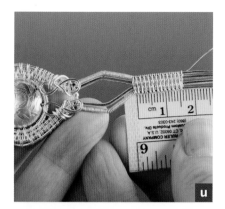

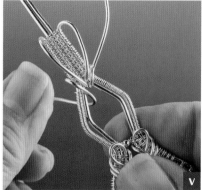

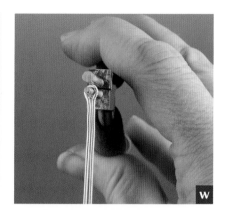

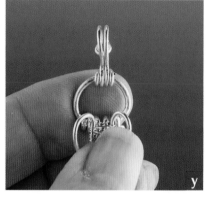

r). Secure the wire end at the back of the weave. Repeat on the opposite side **(photo s)**. Bend the second mark on the remaining frame wires inward. Bend the third mark outward on both wires. String a 3mm metal bead on the weaving wire, and coil the wire to the opposite side and back through the 3mm bead to return the wire to the original position **(photo t)**. Coil the 18-gauge wire on the diamond shape. Once you reach the last bend of the shape with the coil, work in 2-1 weave (see "2-1 Weave," p. 20) with the longer lower frame wire on all four wires for 1.5cm **(photo u)**.

8 / Loop the 18-gauge wires
Bring the 18-gauge frame wires in a forward loop over the 2-1 weave, coil them onto the end of the diamond shape **(photo v)**, and trim and tuck the 18-gauge frame wires to the back.

9 / Solder the clasp rings
Cut 8cm of 16-gauge wire, and coil it onto a 9mm mandrel. Flush-cut the coil

to make two rings. Using easy solder, solder the rings closed.

10 / Coil wire to the soldered ring
Coil the 16-gauge frame wires to the soldered ring twice, and trim and tuck the ends to the back of the weave.

11 / Create the clasp hook
Cut 10cm of 18-gauge wire, and mark the middle of the wire. Using the tip of a roundnose pliers or 2mm bail-forming pliers, form a circle at the mark, keeping the wire ends parallel to each other **(photo w)**. Bend the circled wire into a semi-circle with 3mm bail-forming

pliers. Then, bend the wire ends away from the semi-circle. Arch the wire ends inward and down toward the circle with 3mm bail-forming pliers **(photo x)**. Coil the clasp twice onto the soldered ring on one end of the cuff **(photo y)**. Trim the excess wire.

12 Finish and form the cuff
Warm the piece with a hair dryer, brush on the liver of sulfur, and then rinse thoroughly. Arch the cuff using small hand movements and supporting the entire cuff while slowly manipulating the shape **(photo z)**. Use a bracelet mandrel, if you have one.

design variation
Consider using copper for a cost-effective alternative.

Acknowledgments

Julie (mother) and Art Koogler; two kind souls who filled my life with hope, kindness and constant support. Candy Crawford who opens doors to the minds of those who are highly sensitive to life subtleties. Ruth Ward, who sang her song high upon a roof and showed the world how to follow a dream residing deep within the heart; I delight in this journey with you. To you four people, I bow deeply.

Tela Formosa, the incredible lapidary and fine artist, who made the stunning cabochon on the cover of this book and who mentored me in photography and publication writing, and inspired me artistically.

Erica Barse, editor for Kalmbach Publishing Company, who gave me one of my greatest gifts by paving the path for the opportunity to write this book. Your hard work and constant patience will always be greatly appreciated.

In gratitude to the remarkable professional art team who illuminated the pages of this book: Photography William Zuback; book design Lisa Schroeder, and proof/advisor Annie Pennington.

To those creative souls who walked beside me and fueled my artistic fire: Danielle Ware, Astraea Antal, Margaret Leonard, Dianna Repp, Elizabeth (Elf) Court, Charmaine Allen, Susanne Sheehan, Caroline Cesak, Alex Bacon, Zdzislawa (Gina) Chrzan, Carol Schach, Juanita Brady, and Peggy Burwinkle.

The support I have received from these people is immeasurable: Jimmie Leonard (thank you, daddy), Becky Leonard, James and Dawn Leonard, Kay Barzacchini, Millie Barzacchini, Mike Sheehan, Julie Lockwood Amdal, Fran Zollers and Louis Dries (Score), Dolores Pollitz, Phyllis Stavale, Kim Swigart, Angie Wilderman, Linda Wallace, Florence Hendrickson, Pamela Cozzi, Ronda Bennet, Charlie and Irene Young, James O. Leonard, and Frank and Ruth Repp.

Thank you to ImpressArt. Your stamps and tools illuminate the work of any metal artist.

To burgeoning artists: Ellie, Sienna, and Owen Sheehan, Ellie and Madelyn Leonard, Isabella and Emma Beyke, may you each paint the world with the "artist within" your indelible spirits.

Ron Repp, who is a fabulous author and supportive uncle.

A special thank you to my sister, Pamela Sue Bacon, who is such an encouraging force and one of the most giving people I know.

Thank you to my amazing son, Jonathan Barzacchini, who breathes in nature and breathes out life to all who walk in his wake. Jonathan, you are the light of my life.

And most definitively, a deeply heartfelt thank you to my husband, Mike Barzacchini, who opens his arms and heart, encouraging me to be the person I am meant to be. The gratitude and love I have for you is immense. This world shines brighter with your grace.

About the Author

Susan Barzacchini lives in a northwest suburb of Chicago, East Dundee, Illinois, with her husband, Mike. She is inspired by nature and animals. She has a degree in nursing and cardiac ultrasound, and has a previous history of being a teaching mentor in the medical field for years; teaching is her forte. She has been creating jewelry for two decades and weaving wire for 12 years. Susan has written one of the first Internet tutorials for rolling mill work titled, *From Flat to Fab: Pattern Metals with the Economy Compact Rolling Mill.* She also wrote for *Art Jewelry* magazine and taught at the Bead&Button Show as well as at local colleges and classrooms. She sells her jewelry at Studio V at Harper College in Palatine, Illinois. Cold-connecting wire and metals are her passion, and teaching what she knows about wire is her calling. To see more of Susan's work, visit her website: wiredlotus.com

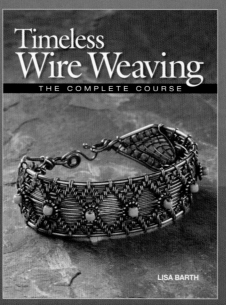
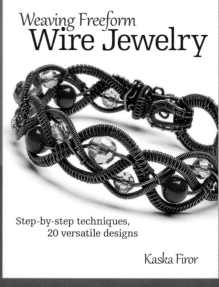